BIOLOGY AND THE RIDDLE OF LIFE

BIOLOGY AND THE RIDDLE OF LIFE

Charles Birch

To Paul Abrecht

A UNSW Press book

Published by
University of New South Wales Press Ltd
University of New South Wales
Sydney 2052 Australia
www.unswpress.com.au

© Charles Birch 1999
First published 1999

National Library of Australia
Cataloguing-in-Publication entry:

Birch, Charles, 1918– .
Biology and the riddle of life.

Bibliography.
Includes index.
ISBN 0 86840 785 2.

1. Biology — Philosophy. 2. Life (Biology). I. Title.

570.1

Printer Griffin Press, Adelaide

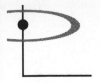

CONTENTS

ACKNOWLEDGMENTS

I dedicate this book to Paul Abrecht who has been a long-time friend and source of many ideas especially on the relation of science and religion and on ethical issues in science. It has been my pleasure to have been a participant in many consultations he has organised in many parts of the world through the World Council of Churches for the past twenty or so years. He will agree on the importance of the issues raised in this book, though he and I have somewhat different metaphysical emphases. This has been to my advantage in challenging my own perspective. I am grateful to Robin Derricourt for his encouragement and to Carl Harrison-Ford for his meticulous scrutiny of my manuscript with the result that it has fewer errors than it otherwise would have had. David Paul kept me abreast of various sources, particularly from the internet, and provided me with an analysis he made of his class of university students for chapter 2. Charles Taylor was particularly helpful in providing me with materials on artificial life and self-organisation for chapter 6. I am much indebted to John B. Cobb for his reading of the manuscript and for his wisdom in guiding me over many years through many philosophical minefields.

INTRODUCTION

In the 1990s, going into the new millennium, biology overtook physics in the news. From genetic engineering to cloning to ecology, biology made news. Physics for a long time has been regarded as the fundamental science. But is the epigram of John Scott Haldane now coming true? 'If physics and biology one day meet, and one of the two is swallowed up, that one will not be biology' (Needham 1943 p. 204). One of the most quoted passages of A. N. Whitehead was that in which he said: 'Science is taking on a new aspect which is neither purely physical, nor purely biological. It is becoming the study of organisms. Biology is the study of larger organisms, whereas physics is the study of smaller organisms' (Whitehead 1925 p. 129). This is an idea whose time has come. A central argument of this book is that science is destined more and more to take on the role of studying its entities, be they protons or people, as organisms. An embracing biology can now provide the basic philosophical framework within which to form a picture of our own nature and that of all the rest of nature. Considerable attention is given in this book to the meaning of this radical proposition.

There is today a strange paradox about the science of life. Despite its dominance in science news it is most reluctant to define for us what its subject matter is—namely life! Some of the reasons for this are discussed in chapter 1. Yet much of modern biology, especially in the writings of its popular exponents, such as Richard Dawkins in England and Stephen Jay Gould in the USA, conveys the impression that modern biology explains, or is about to explain, all that is to be known about life. Their explanation, though widely differing in details, is a mechanistic model, not an organismic one which I explain in chapter 3.

The mechanistic model of life has led to the publication of many books and articles that claim to tell us 'the secret of life'. Most of these tell us that DNA is the secret of life. The story goes that Francis Crick, the co-discoverer of the structure of DNA, on that famous day ran into a Cambridge pub to announce that he had discovered 'the secret of life'. It would be truer to say that DNA is one of many secrets of life. It is a necessary but not sufficient explanation. You can sit DNA in a test tube forever and it won't come to life. It won't even replicate. It has to be plugged into a complex network of physics and chemistry before it exhibits its remarkable properties. We no longer think of DNA as the initiating molecule of life but as a step along the way. The potential for life as we know it existed from the foundations of the universe. DNA happens to be one necessary step for making that potential concretely real. Ian Stewart (1998) argues that life has another secret which is mathematics. Indeed, many of the ordered systems of living organisms that he discusses have a mathematical basis, some of which are discussed in chapter 6. Yet other 'secrets of life' are discussed elsewhere in this book.

A proposition of this book is that from its foundations biology has had a superb history in explaining the objective aspects of life, that is, the things that can be weighed and measured such as muscular contraction or nerve impulses or the order of the seeds in a sunflower head. It has been very clever in explaining things as mechanisms. But so-called scientific objectivity has been unable to deal with the subjective aspects of life, with subjects as such—what it is like to be alive, what it is like to have a toothache, what it is like to be in love. There seem to be hidden secrets there which suggest that the time is ripe to move from the model of mechanism to that of organism, for the model of organism includes the subjective. Latterly Dawkins (1998) has indicated his recognition of the subjective as a problem when he says: 'The problems raised by subjective consciousness are perhaps the most baffling in all philosophy, and solving them is far beyond my ambition' (p. 283). But why avoid this issue so central to what life is about? In a similar vein, several contributors to the book *Consciousness and Human Identity* edited by John Cornwell (1998) adopt the attitude that the problem of the subjective, or understanding living creatures as subjects, is intractable because the way we think in the modern science of biology is 'not commensurable' with such issues.

One object of this book is to suggest an approach to understanding the living organism that is commensurable with what we know about the subjective in our lives and in the lives of of other creatures. Indeed, that recognition calls for a radical extension of science as we usually think of it. This book calls for a recognition by science of a wider field of exploration that includes the subjective. That is, to study organisms as organisms. The time has come for science to march to another drummer. Only then will biology be in a position to speak to physics and vice versa. 'The doctrine that I am maintaining,' said Whitehead (1938), 'is that neither physical nature nor life can be understood unless we fuse them together as factors in the composition of "really real" things whose interconnections and individual characters constitute the universe' (p. 150). He went on to say that the deficiencies in our concept of physical nature should be supplied by its fusion with life and the notion of life should involve the notion of physical nature. He was implying the radical notion that without a subject there can be no object.

This objective will not be achieved by one set of people, call them scientists or what you will, investigating the objective while another group such as philosophers and theologians investigate the subjective. It is possible and necessary for the one mind to embrace both and fuse them into one rational scheme of thought. That is why A. N. Whitehead (1861–1947), who achieved this, can be so important in our thinking and why I make many references to him. He was scientist, philosopher and theologian. His life was first spent in Cambridge, then London, and later at Harvard. Whitehead's most important book, *Process and Reality* (1929a; rev. 1978) were his Gifford Lectures. This book, despite many very difficult passages, has been compared to the achievements of Plato. Whitehead described this work as speculative philosophy which he defined as 'the endeavour to frame a coherent, logical, necessary system of general ideas in terms of which every element of our experience can be interpreted' (p. 3). As I indicate in chapter 1 this genre of thought is part of a stream of thought that goes back to Ikhnaton in Egypt and Plato in Greece and has a rich flowering in out time through Whitehead and his followers who incorporate in that stream the thought of the scientific revolution in its modern form. I would like to think that this book may persuade its readers to drink from that stream.

Biologists are good at recognising objective correlates of our various experiences that can be measured, such as the quantities and kinds of hormones released into our bloodstream when in love or in the nature of the nerve impulses involved in depression. But there is also a subjective aspect of being alive. This is what it is like to be someone with aches and pains and joys and sufferings. It is the first-person aspect as distinguished from the third-person aspect of objective science. There is a tremendous gap between what biology, as we known it, describes and our own experience. Some biologists deny that there is any subjective aspect that cannot in principle be reduced to the objective, that all will eventually be reduced to the objective. This dilemma is discussed in chapter 3.

The idea of two perspectives on life is contained in the famous and wonderful parable of the cave in Plato's *Republic*. Human beings are like prisoners chained to the wall of a dark subterranean cave, where they can never turn around to see the light of a fire that is higher up and at a distance behind them. Objects outside the cave pass on a parapet like the screen of a puppet show. The parapet is in front of the fire. The prisoners can only see shadows of the objects cast on the wall in front of them. They mistake the shadows for reality. Only one who is freed from his chains and leaves the cave to enter the world beyond can glimpse true reality, though when first exposed to the light such a one may be overwhelmed with its dazzlingly luminosity. Yet once this person habituates to the light and comes to recognise the true nature of things his understanding is transformed. He then holds precious the clarity of his new understanding. Recalling his former fate among the prisoners, where all necessarily devote their minds to the understanding of mere illusions, he would prefer anything in the real world than be forced to live in the underworld of shadows. Indeed, were he required to return to the cave and, unaccustomed to its darkness, contend with the others in their shadow world, he would only provoke their ridicule.

For Plato the parable of the cave concerned the task of the philosopher as he understood it, to emerge from the cave of ephemeral shadows and bring his darkened mind into the light that is the source of his being, the light of transcendent truth, goodness and beauty. I am using the parable in a somewhat different context. There are two views of what life is. To see life only in terms of a mechanist view is to live in a degree of darkness. We need more light. Science's laboratory is a cave in which a great deal is achieved, but this understanding needs to be brought into another light which is illuminating in a different sort of way. This is the first-person enlightenment of my private experience in contrast to the third-person enlightenment that science gives me. So in my interpretation the scientist and those who follow need to get out into another light, from thence to return again to the cave to do more work, hopefully with a new and stereoscopic perspective. And then ultimately to work all the time in the bright light with stereoscopic vision.

A specific example of what I mean is the present study of consciousness by top-flight biologists around the world. They are telling us a great deal of the processes that go on in the brain when we are conscious but they leave untouched the problem of qualia, which is a technical term referring to the experiential (first person) qualities of sensations. How to bring the two together is largely left to philosophers such as Searle (1997) and Griffin (1998). This bringing together is also the object of this book. It is what the philosophy of organism is all about. It involves excursions of thought in what these days is being called metascience and in earlier times metaphysics. The prefix *meta* means beyond.

The parable of the cave can be told in a more modern form as a movie shown in a dark theatre. The objects that appear on the screen are the result of a film strip passing in front of a bright light which casts pictures on the screen. We may learn a lot in the cave of the theatre about life but what is on the screen is not life. There is nothing alive there at all. We get a perspective on life from the movie picture, but it is not life. In the days of silent black-and-white movies we got a perspective on life but it was a less real one than watching a colour movie with sound. The scientific picture of life is the movie. It is getting better and better in detail each year and so it tells us a more complete story each year. We learn a lot from it. But it is still not the real thing because it is not the complete story. The pictures of people on the screen do not have any feelings. They portray people who did have feelings when they were being photographed. This incompleteness of the film as a depiction of life is one reason why biology is reluctant to define what life is.

There is a growing awareness that science does not require a completely mechanistic worldview. The question is then asked: what further descriptions do we need, in addition to those with which science provides us? It has been my conviction for a large part of my life that a more complete image of life and its meaning is given in the perspective of what has been known as process thought. This is another name for what Whitehead called the philosophy of organism. This taught me a new way of looking at the world, a new way of raising questions. The word 'process' refers to the proposition that the individual entities of the world, from protons to people, are not to be thought of as things like solid matter but as events or processes. This is to make a fundamental shift from a substance view of the world to an event view. That is not to say that a proton or an atom is something first that then acts. It is to say that these individual entities are themselves events and not substances at all. Much of this book is concerned with the nature of this activity. This view is consistent with what is now known as the new physics, so clearly explained by Davies and Gribbin (1991) in their refutation of what they call 'the matter myth'. Physicists got out of the cave, at least they poked their heads out, before biologists.

In the view of process thought there is a second proposition that concerns the nature of the events that constitute a proton or a person which gives us the clue to why Whitehead called this the philosophy of organism. The fundamental process of being an entity, be it that of a proton or a person, is a process of experiencing. This is a much more controversial proposition. The word 'experience' used for a proton is by analogy with the meaning we understand for our own conscious experiences. It is not to say that protons think or are conscious. Far from it. Our recognition of mind at a late stage in the process of evolution is evidence that mind must be in some manner present from the first. It is implicit in that from which it comes. The meaning of this view and evidence for it are discussed in some detail in later chapters. We tend to thingify the world when ours is an experiential world. In this sense all individual entities from protons to people are experiential. Hence the term panexperientialism, which is a name process thought now gives to this way of looking at things. The final chapter on this book suggests how the process view can also lead to a naturalistic understanding of theism, though the God of process theism is very different from the interventionist supernatural God of much current religion.

And what about wonder and mystery? A philosophical and stereoscopic perspective of science and all experience increases both wonder and mystery. It lights up the world and yet points to a world beyond, still veiled in degrees of darkness. This is certainly true of a process view. For some scientists that happens even when their science is exclusively mechanistic. Richard Dawkins (1998) has written a whole book about that in defence of the charge that his is a bleak and cold view of reality. Ursula Goodenough (1998) is another biologist who finds, even in reductionist biology, a source of solace and hope that leads in her case to mysticism. Wonder and mystery are part and parcel of a scientific attitude. Alone they do not lead to a synthesis of the objective and the subjective in a philosophy of organism which, I argue, is the important step for science to take. In doing this I am reminded of a plea of Bill Coffin who was the dynamic and radical pastor of the famous inclusive Riverside Church in New York, whose thinking was also inclusive. His church drew many of its members from neighbouring Columbia University and Harlem. He used to remind his flock that in their search for understanding together they should seek not certainty but clarity. Certainty is a fake. Conviction with clarity is for real—deep yet clear:

> Oh, could I flow like thee, and make thy stream
> My great example, as it is my theme!
> Though deep, yet clear; though gentle, not yet dull;
> Strong without rage, without o'erflowing full.

John Denham, *Cooper's Hill*

1

WHAT IS LIFE?

As for life, I suspect that, twenty years hence, biologists may be concerning themselves with 'the question of life' just as vigorously as the rest of us now are with problems about consciousness.

Mary Midgley (1996 p. 502)

Books on biology until recently usually commenced with a definition of life. Today one looks for a definition of life in modern texts on biology to no avail. A recent compendium by several authors entitled *What is Life?* (Murphy & O'Neill 1995) is equally reluctant to provide any definitive answer to the question. I remember Nobel prizeman Sir Peter Medawar saying in conversation, 'life is an abstract noun never used in laboratories'. Another Nobel prizeman, Albert Szent-Gyorgyi, said 'Every biologist has at some time asked "What is life?" and none has ever given a satisfactory answer' (Szent-Gyorgyi 1972). Bob Holmes (1998) found this to be the case when he phoned many of his biological colleagues for an answer. He said he felt like a sportswriter ringing up coaches and asking them to define the game of football. It seems that biologists are quite reluctant to define life. The reasons for this are suggested later in this chapter. Standard dictionaries of biology do not have an entry for this word. Those biologists who occasionally mention it refer only to a few formal qualities such as reproduction, complexity, mutation and metabolism. None of these is life. It is rather ridiculous to say 'life is complexity', as I have heard one computer modeller say. It may be true to say that a living cell is more complex than an atom, but even that statement is not without its difficulties, as is discussed in chapter 6.

Yet the question, what is life? did become an important one for NASA, whose space vehicles went in search of life on other planets. What did they look for? The first effort was on Mars and the problem was to design a machine that could detect life. There were many suggestions. One was to send a kind of microscope with a long sticky tongue that would unroll on the surface of the planet. It would then roll back and put whatever dust it found under the microscope. Images would be sent back to Earth. If something wiggles then it is alive. A more sophisticated approach was taken. Instead of asking whether things on Mars looked alive, it was decided to ask whether they have the metabolism of living things. The Mars Lander contained a long hose attached to a sort of vacuum cleaner inside of which was a container of radioactive growth-medium. When the Lander got to Mars it would suck up some dust into the medium. If there were any living organism there they would break down the medium as bacteria do. Radioactive carbon dioxide would be produced and a detector in the machine would signal its presence to Earth. And that is exactly what happened. Radioactive carbon dioxide was produced, convincing everyone that they had found life on Mars. But then suddenly the process shut down. Apparently there was a kind of chemical reaction on finely divided clay particles which was not ordinarily seen on Earth. Later this reaction was successfully mimicked in the laboratory, so everybody agreed there was no life on Mars. What the Mars Lander really told us was that there was no Earth-like bacterial life on Mars.

More recent propositions have been to look for certain chemicals or chemical reactions characteristic of life on Earth. But again the problem is that you may find some chemical reaction that mimics life but is not alive. There are lot of people trying to create life in a test tube (see Davies 1998 chaps 3 and 5). If they succeed we might be in a better position to define what life is. But that is some distance down the track. All these efforts are directed to discovering 'life as we know it'. But we cannot rule out the possibility that in some other part of the universe there may exist 'life as we do not know it' based, say, on silicon atoms instead of carbon.

Another approach to defining life has been that of artificial life discussed in chapter 6. The essence of this approach is to create artificial life in a computer. In one example the 'organisms' are packets of computer code designed to make copies of themselves with occasional changes like genetic mutations. 'I'd say it's alive,' said Thomas Ray, who produces such programs (Holmes 1998 p. 42). But his creatures consist not of proteins and nucleic acids but of 1's and 0's on a silicon chip. 'It is as far from life as dolls are from babies,' says Lynn Margulis. It seems that it is a matter of choice as to which definition of life is most useful in the field we happen to be working in, be it searching for life on other planets or in computer programs or trying to make life in the biochemist's laboratory.

Nobel Prize physicist Erwin Schrodinger wrote a book in 1944 with the title *What is Life?* It has been described as one of the most influential books in the history of science. Its object was to investigate the extent to which life could be accounted for in terms of physics and chemistry, despite our 'obvious inability' to define life. He had two themes—'order from disorder' and 'order from order'. Order from disorder emphasised that life fed on negative entropy, which is a way of saying that whereas the universe as a whole is becoming less ordered (positive entropy) life creates greater order (negative entropy). This is not an exception to the rule of the universe for the rule simply says that, whereas the universe as a whole is running down, there are enclaves where the opposite may happen and one such enclave is living organisms. There is nothing mysterious about this. Living organisms get their necessary energy to do this from the sun. The sun's energy is trapped by plants. Animals get their energy by feeding on plants. Maybe this notion was little appreciated at the time that Schrodinger wrote. It is thought that he probably got the idea from a lecture which he heard in Vienna in 1886 by the physicist Ludwig Boltzmann.

Schrodinger's second principle of 'order from order' was about how information was passed on from generation to generation by genes. He predicted the general nature of the gene more than a decade before the structure of DNA was understood. The importance of Schrodinger's book was that it drew several of the brightest physicists of the day into biology. These were the scientists who eventually helped to solve some of the problems in terms of what happens at the molecular level.

Fifty years after the publication of Schrodinger's book, a group of biologists got together to celebrate its publication and to speculate about the next fifty years of biology (Murphy & O'Neill 1995). Curiously they saw progress in the future understanding of life as running along the Schrodinger track of mechanistic biology which seeks to interpret life solely in terms of physics and chemistry. A. N. Whitehead long ago anticipated that biology would take over physics and not physics take over biology. But that has not happened. That it could happen is one of the propositions of this book, for physics and chemistry as we know them do not account for the full richness of biological phenomena, notably our experiences.

WHEN LIFE SLIPS THROUGH OUR FINGERS

Despite recent discoveries extending from molecular biology to ecology, it seems that life simply slips through the biologist's fingers. Why? A thesis of this book is that there is more to life than physics and chemistry as we know them. Modern science has developed close ties to materialism, also known as physicalism. All reality, says the materialist or physicalist, is material. Humans are nothing but machines. Life is nothing but chemical reactions. Consciousness is nothing but a phenomenon soon to be explained in physical and chemical terms. These are all 'nothing but' philosophies. But did any one of us ever think of his or her own life in such terms? Certainly not those who find their lives most meaningfully described in terms of pleasure and pain, interest and boredom, love and hate and all those other phenomena that remain for us as the most important consequences of being alive. So philosopher John Searle (1997) wrote:

> Once you have described the facts about my body and my brain, for example, you still seem to have a lot of facts left over about my beliefs, desires, pains, etc. Materialists typically think they have to get rid of these mental facts by reducing them to material phenomena or by showing that they don't really exist at all. (p. 43)

Physiologist Sir John Eccles remarked at a meeting of biologists and philosophers on just this subject: 'I'll be reduced to physics and chemistry only when I'm dead' (Goodfield 1972 p. 448). And geneticist Steve Jones (1997a) said: 'When it comes to sex—or history, or politics, or opera—science can answer all questions except the interesting ones' (p. 41). The trouble with the modern worldview is that so many aspects of being alive—emotional, aesthetic, ethical, volitional, relational, imaginative—are regarded as irrelevant or distortional for an objective understanding of the real world. The dominant modern worldview, which is probably unprecedented in Western society, is of a world devoid of purpose, ruled by chance and necessity, without intrinsic meaning or value. It is quite unable to deal with the question, what is life? But some scientists right now are asking big questions that could lead in another direction.

THE BIG QUESTIONS

A hundred or so well-known scientists, plus a few engineers and high-tech entrepreneurs, were e-mailed with this quite simple question: what questions are you asking yourself? The resulting responses can be found at the 'World Question Center' on the Internet. An editorial in the *New Scientist* commented: 'Surprisingly, it turns out that only a few scientists are totally taken up with the daily concerns of their narrow sub-discipline. Rather more seem a bit too worried about the conventional Big Problems of the destruction of the environment, the world's growing population, or the shocking effects of a materialistic society on young people' (7 February 1998 p.3). The editorial went on to say that the majority of those approached asked big, deep and ambitious questions that suggest that science is edging into the domain of philosophy and religion. Here are some of those questions from 'The World Question Center':

> Is the universe a great mechanism, a great computation, a great symmetry, a great accident, or a great thought?
> What is the crucial distinction between inanimate matter and an entity [the human being] which can act at as 'agent' manipulating the world on its own behalf?
> Are the most remarkable things in life—sights, sounds, colours, tastes—really just subjective epiphenomena with no role or significance in the 'objective' world?
> How can we develop an objective language for describing subjective experience?
> Are life and consciousness purely emergent phenomena, or subtly connected to a fundamental level of the universe?
> What is life and what makes us special?

These questions suggest that those who ask them are unsatisfied with traditional answers to the big questions, even those coming from science. Every second year in the 1990s over a thousand professional people have met at Tucson, Arizona, to spend a week or so listening to papers on consciousness. They include biologists, philosophers, psychologists, new agers and others. At Tucson 2 1000 questionnaires were distributed with about 200 being completed. The idea was to get some idea of the background ideas of the participants. The results were surprising. Some 93 per cent said they 'think about the ultimate meaning of life'. Some 66 per cent said they have had 'experiences which science would have difficulty in explaining'. Some 72 per cent said they 'feel a need to find a real meaning and purpose in life'. Only 24 per cent said there is 'no reality other than the physical universe'. There were many other questions. All in all, the responses suggested a deep interest in the meaning of life, an uncertainty of the ability of science as we know it to help in answering these questions, and a sense that a lot of questions as yet have no answer. The analysis unfortunately did not indicate how representative the sample was of the different fields of interest of the participants but it did indicate that amongst those interested enough to return the questionnaire there was a deep interest in the big questions and the unsolved dilemmas (Baruss & Moore 1998).

Martin Gardner (1996) quotes Lewis Thomas' proposal that the best way to interest young people in science is to teach not only what is known, but also what is unknown. There should be courses, he suggested, that dealt systematically with ignorance and 'informed bewilderment' (p. 554). This could lead to three possible outcomes:

One is the discovery of problems that science may yet elucidate. This was well exemplified when physicists joined the ranks of biologists to invent molecular biology. What happened? Because of their different background and knowledge the physicists brought new ideas, information and new techniques to the problem which opened up vast new fields of research.

A second outcome is that some questions cannot yield to our present methods of science and need the discovery of a different approach and the defining of new questions, perhaps more philosophical ones as distinct from the questions that led to molecular biology. Discovery consists in seeing what everybody has seen and thinking what nobody has thought. The statement that science can in principle discover everything can only be defended when it is reduced to the tautology that science can discover anything which science is capable of discovering. There are some things for which science, as we at present know it, does not lead to provision of answers. Such questions are referred to later in this chapter. There is no way science as practised can answer Stephen Hawking's question of, as he put it, 'why the universe bothers to exist'.

A third outcome is that there are some questions we ask that may not in principle be answered by science or anything else. I had never thought seriously about this third position until I met a philosopher who described his position as 'commonsense noumenism'. This word refers to Immanuel Kant's *noumena* which are the unknowable realities behind the *phenomena* of our experience. The noumenist philosopher said to me that he regarded consciousness as a phenomenon that cannot in principle be explained. In regard to that problem we are, he suggested, just like a cockroach who will never be able to explain Newton's laws of motion. Our plummet line is too short to reach such depths.

In summary, a recognition of ignorance can lead to discovery, it can lead to the implementation of new philosophical methods, and it can help us to recognise questions not yet answerable with our present tools or maybe with any tools.

THE HARD PROBLEM

When asked what he would say if, when he died, he found that there was a God, Bertrand Russell replied that he would ask: 'why did you not give us the data Lord?' Some problems in science and philosophy are really hard nuts to crack. For some of them this is because we think that the answers can only come from a specialist approach to gather more data. The scientist is expected to be a specialist in, say, quarks or may be the circulatory system of snails. Many, perhaps most, cling to professional standards as lifebelts to keep afloat in a sea of disconnected facts in which they have lost the capacity to swim, let alone to plumb the depths. To change the metaphor, they religiously visit every station of the old mechanistic cross.

A ready way to make enemies amongst one's scientific colleagues is to suggest that the traditional framework of thinking in science is not adequate to solving some of the really hard problems. Of course one approach to the hard problems is to avoid them. Indeed if you want to get a Nobel Prize you choose to work on tractable problems that yield to the normal methods of scientific investigation. Our PhD students have to work on research problems that can be resolved within about three years. Though they may think otherwise, the really hard problems are not for them, not yet at any rate. Some curbing of interest may be necessary, as in the case of the student who presented a manuscript to his professor with the statement: 'This is my first book. It explains the universe.' One wonders what the subject of his second book might be! The professor doesn't have to be too much of a wet blanket. A young graduate student brought his first paper to the professor to look at before he sent it away for publication. The professor read it, looked wearily at his student and said: 'You have heard the saying, publish or perish. Young man, you have made the wrong choice!' A more gentle approach is called for. Early in my life as a teacher I learned from a mentor: never try to discourage a student, you will almost always be successful.

We have to steer apprentice research students away from knocking their brains out on the really hard problems. Scientists are deliberately trained to deal with the easy problems first. But this approach doesn't have to last for ever. Otherwise they could miss out on one of the great excitements of knowledge, which is getting out of the specialist trench we dig ourselves into to look over the edges to exciting fields beyond.

The most difficult problem being tackled in biology today is the problem of consciousness or feelings. Exploring the physiology of vision is 'easy'. Understanding the subjective visual experience, say that of seeing green, is 'hard'. Many biologists, perhaps most, who deal with such problems, say there is no such thing as a hard problem about consciousness. All can be eventually reduced to chemical reactions in nerve cells. But there are dissenters. I am one of them.

Experience, we say, is an irreducible phenomenon, inscrutable for standard mechanistic reductionist science. Mentality may even be, as one of the questions above suggested, a fundamental aspect of all matter, not just the matter of nerve cells. The most emphatic expression of this radical view is Whitehead's (1929a) statement 'apart from the experience of subjects there is nothing, nothing, nothing, bare nothingness'! (p. 167). This he calls the reformed subjectivist principle. The stuff of the world, proposes Whitehead, is mind stuff. If that happens to be true of the world, then clearly we would never crack the nature of nature if we proceeded on our specialist reductionist path of regular science alone, which sees all as machinery.

Here is an example of how this divide manifests itself, even between great investigators. Two of the greatest polymaths of this century were Bertrand Russell and Alfred North Whitehead. For ten years they cooperated in writing the monumental *Principia Mathematica*. For them that was an easy problem. Then they parted company. Russell became a leading exponent of a materialistic philosophy, yet one sensitive to social values. All problems were easy problems. Whitehead rejected materialism and with it the dominant interpretation of science, which is mechanistic, for what he called an organic view of the universe. Russell said that either life is matter-like or matter is life-like. He chose the former—life is matter-like. Whitehead chose the latter—matter is life-like. Whitehead introduced Russell at a lecture at Harvard University as follows: 'Bertie says that I am muddle-headed. But I think he is simple-minded.' Here we have the contrast stated in succinct terms. There are those who would be clear and neat by oversimplifying. For them there are no hard problems. 'Seek simplicity' is the catchphrase. Well and good, said Whitehead, but distrust it. On the other hand there are those who would accept the many-sidedness of reality, including its mystery, even if they cannot always be neat and clear in their account of it. You can have a philosophy of life which throws much light on understanding without claiming that it explains everything. Nothing does.

When William Blake decried what he called 'Newton's sleep' he accepted science's separate existence, but believed that its adherents were blinkered. They failed to see the hard problems. This attack was carried forward in the 'two cultures' debate of thirty-five years ago. The debate was resurrected in the symbolism of the statue of Newton, based on Blake's vision, that fronts the new building of the British Library in London. The library had for several years been wrapped like a birthday present awaiting its long-delayed opening, perhaps a far from subtle comment on the position of knowledge of all kinds today, wrapped up waiting to be revealed.

A very different statue of Newton was erected in 1775 in the Temple of Worthies by the British government. The inscription reads: 'Sir Isaac Newton, Whom the God of Nature made to comprehend his works: and from simple Principles, to discover the laws never before known.' Correct, but not of the literary merit of Alexander Pope who said:

Nature and Nature's Laws lay hid in night:
God said, *Let Newton be!* and all was light.

Well, not quite all, for the problem was a harder one than Newton's machine-like universe could solve. He was blinkered about that. We had to await Einstein to show that was the case. Relativity began to crack the hard problems of physics, then later on came quantum physics which is still struggling. Biology right now awaits its Einstein for an answer to the question, what is life?

I have for long been baffled trying to relate the simple vision of science to a larger reality that includes philosophy, religion and the arts. The light came to me when I first read Whitehead's (1925) chapter 5, entitled 'The Romantic Reaction' in his *Science and the Modern World*. That opened my eyes to the importance of distinguishing between the easy and the hard problems. This isn't just an academic issue. In the nineteenth century John Stuart Mill was brought up by his father to become a thinking machine. He suffered a nervous breakdown at the age of twenty. He then turned to the poetry of Wordsworth (as did Whitehead), which rescued him from depression and tapped a vein of deep feeling which had been scanted by his education.

Whitehead (1929a) made the following provocative statement which really irritates the traditional scientist: 'In the real world it is more important that a proposition be interesting than that it be true. The importance of truth is that it adds to interest' (p. 259). He was not saying that truth was unimportant. He was saying that the important thing was to be interesting and that would lead to truth. Interest is the mainspring of life and thought. Who is going to be interested in truth if the truth is uninteresting? People don't normally want mere information as such. They want interesting information. They want answers to questions worth asking. If they are given any other kind of information they usually can't remember it. When someone tells me that was an interesting lecture you gave yesterday I ask in response, what did you find interesting? Sometimes I get a blank stare or at most they can remember a joke I told. Their problem is that they have no mental pegs onto which to hang new information.

If they had there would have been important questions hanging on some mental peg or other that was crying out for an answer.

A task today, particularly in the science of life, is to make interesting propositions, especially way-out ones. Physicist John A. Wheeler said to his students, 'If you haven't found something strange during the day it hasn't been much of a day.' He encouraged that attitude amongst his students. One of them in response to his teacher did let his ideas get a bit out of hand. Professor Wheeler said to him, 'I can't believe space is that crummy'. Noting the fallen expression on the student's face Wheeler touched his arm and added encouragingly: 'To disagree leads to study, to study leads to understanding, to understand is to appreciate, to appreciate is to love. So maybe I'll end up loving your theory.'

THE FALLACY OF THE PERFECT DICTIONARY

There is a belief by some that humanity has thought up all the fundamental ideas about life and its meaning. Further it is held that language in single words or phrases explicitly expresses these ideas. Whitehead (1938 p. 173) calls this The Fallacy of the Perfect Dictionary. It is to lack the power of delicate accuracy of expression. I remember, to my chagrin, asking Sir Karl Popper what was his definition of mind. He replied, in no uncertain terms, that it was no way to start a serious discussion by defining terms. Once you do that you give the impression that you know the answer before you have started. On another occasion Popper said that when people ask him to define a word he has used, he usually instead proposes a different word. When we ask the question, what is life? we soon realise that a simple definition will get us nowhere. What the question can do is to initiate a discussion of a complex issue that may bring us to a greater understanding of the question than we had when we began the discussion. Blaise Pascal said, '*Le dieu defini est le dieu fini*'. How can you define something that is infinite in finite terms?

The fallacy of the perfect dictionary divides philosophy, said Whitehead (1938 p. 173), into two schools; the critical school and the speculative school. The critical school confines itself to verbal analysis within the limits of the dictionary. The speculative school enlarges the dictionary by exploring meanings and seeking further insights. It is willing to have an attitude of adventure in the face of mystery and ignorance. The divergence between the two is, suggests Whitehead, the quarrel between safety and adventure.

The history of the quantum theory in physics is not a succession of clear-cut ideas. This is illustrated by a discussion in 1958 between two great physicists, Werner Heisenberg and Wolfgang Pauli, in which they put forward an unorthodox theory of particles. This group of physicists included another great physicist, Niels Bohr. In the discussion, younger scientists were sharply critical of Pauli. Bohr rose to speak. 'We are all agreed,' he said to Pauli, 'that your theory is crazy. The question which divides us is whether it is crazy enough to have a chance of being correct.' The objection that Pauli and Heisenberg were not crazy enough, says Freeman Dyson, applies to all attempts to launch a radically new theory of elementary particles (from Gardner 1996 p. 79). Whitehead (1925) said: 'Almost all really new ideas have a certain aspect of foolishness when they are first produced' (p. 60). I think it was T. H. Huxley who, thinking of Darwinism, said 'It is the fate of new truths to begin as heresies'. Some end up as superstitions!

ALIVENESS

The question I am interested in about life is this: what does science explain about life and what if anything comes into the category of escaping the scientific analysis as we known it? An example of the latter is the problem of aliveness. In chapter 2 I indicate the extent to which science helps us here. For the moment I want to outline some of the issues that have not yielded to scientific analysis but yet are not in the category of the completely unknowable. There is so much that we do not known that it behoves us to recognise the extent of our ignorance as well as the extent of our knowledge. There is a Buddhist text that says: 'If there were as many Ganges Rivers as there are grains of sand in the Ganges and again as many Ganges Rivers as there are grains of sand in those new Ganges Rivers, then the number of grains of sand would be smaller than the number of things not known by the Buddha'. Knowledge is like blowing up a big balloon. The bigger it becomes the more of the unknown it comes into contact with. The more we know the more there is to be known.

My thesaurus gives the following alternative associated words for 'alive': vital, energetic, ardent, eager, spirited, intense, vigorous. Its antonyms are: dead, inert, inanimate, defunct, sluggish, dull, vapid. So aliveness is to be intense and vigorous. Non-aliveness is to be sluggish, dull or dead. For clues to aliveness I look not to physics nor even biology but to an apprehension of my own aliveness. This puts on its head the proposition that we begin by knowing all about the ultimate constituents of the inorganic world and then ask whether they can account for the observable phenomena of living things.

Because this latter approach left the phenomenon of life out in the cold, a movement developed last century called vitalism. This was the doctrine that living things had something in addition to atoms and molecules called vital spirits, the *elan vital* or some such. In general terms vitalism proposed that living things consist of an X in addition to carbon, hydrogen, oxygen, nitrogen, etc. Vitalism is dead. It expired about 1930.

Contrasted to vitalism and pure mechanism is a third concept— the organismic concept. It claims that we do not know about atoms and molecules until we discover what they become in their most complex arrangements, which are in living organisms. When it turns out that certain arrangements of the atoms of carbon, hydrogen, oxygen and so on exhibit properties such as we recognise by the name of enzymes, when even more complex arrangements result in brains which we recognise as conscious, we have discovered something about atoms and molecules we did not know before. So the proposition of this organic view is that in addition to starting with atoms and molecules (the bottom up approach) we also start with what they become in the complex living organism (the top down approach).

This means we start with the reality of our subjective lives. Biology as such has very little to say about that for it has traditionally investigated living organisms as machines. It analyses living creatures as objects (not subjects). This is the objective or bottom-up approach It tells us about the heart as a pump and the limbs as levers operated by muscles and tendons and genes as complex molecules that set specific chemical reactions in chain. It has very little to say about our subjective feelings. It can tell us a lot about the physiological chain of events when we see the colour green, from the reception of light by the light-sensitive cells of the retina at the back of the eye to the electrical transmission through the optic nerve to the brain. But it leaves out the subjective sensation we actually experience of seeing green or feeling courageous. It tells us much about the biological correlates of sensation but nothing about the sensation itself.

We are subjects and not just objects. We are organisms and not just mechanisms. The word 'subject' comes from a Latin word which literally means 'thrown under'. It means the underlying reality of things. Aliveness refers to the underlying reality of being alive and that has to do with experiences or feelings. It has to do with what it is like to *be* something. What is like to be a bat? Or what is it like to be a human? To be a subject, says Thomas Nagel (1974), is to have a particular personal point of view of the world, to know the world from the *inside*. It is to have a first-person perspective, what is it like to *be*. By contrast the objective perspective is the third-person perspective. It is to see from the outside and so to see an object. Science typically deals with the objective which, in the terms of science, is that which can be measured. And in so dealing with the objective side of things science has been eminently successful from the astronomy of Copernicus to the molecular biology of Watson and Crick. From the sixteenth century onwards mechanism was the magic secret which unsnarled all tangles and solved all mysteries. Human life, indeed all life, is an affair of machinery. The out and out materialist says it is nothing but machinery, complex though that machinery may be. It is increasingly incredible to commonsense that the only things that have any importance, namely feelings and qualities, are the things to be omitted from 'reality', that the real is unimportant and the important is unreal. This I say cannot be true. Here then are some alternative propositions from another perspective:

My first proposition is that the most real thing about life is not its machinery but the subjective experience of feeling aliveness, that life strives for ever more aliveness and that when that striving ceases we are for dead. There are degrees of aliveness and there are degrees of deadness. Hamlet experienced both ends of the spectrum. In Act 1 he says:

> What a piece of work is a man! How noble in reason! How infinite in faculty! ... in action how like an angel! in apprehension how like a God! the beauty of the world! the paragon of animals! And yet to me, what is this quintessence of dust?

And his response to this question Hamlet describes his state of being at the dead end of his experiential spectrum:

> O! that this too too solid flesh would melt,
> Thaw, and resolve itself into a dew;
> Or that the Everlasting had not fix'd
> His canon 'gainst self-slaughter! O God! O God!
> How weary, stale, flat, and unprofitable
> Seem to me all the uses of this world.

Biologist Lewis Wolpert (1999) wrote a book on his severe depression and recovery. To give an inkling of the devastation he experienced he quoted Anne Sexton's poem 'The Sickness Unto Death':

> God went out of me
> as if the sea dried up like sandpaper
> as if the sun became a latrine
> God went out of my fingers.
> They became stone.

A person may be very much alive today but tomorrow in a state of depression or partial deadness. Or one state may be dominant over the other. I am always surprised in reading of the lives of the great to discover how their lives were very much a mixture of aliveness with deadly depression intervening at points along the course.

Theologian Paul Tillich himself confessed that 'every morning from seven till ten I live with the demons'. By demons he meant that which divided his life and caused an estrangement from what he could be. In an account of the lives of seven gurus including Jung and Freud, the psychiatrist Anthony Storr (1997) points out that each one experienced a 'dark night of the soul' before discovering enlightenment. Storr refers to this experience as a 'creative illness'. For example, Carl Gustav Jung spoke of a mid-life crisis when for years he was 'menaced by a psychosis'. He withdrew from teaching at the university and found himself unable to read scientific literature. He felt his house was crowded with spirits of the dead. Yet he said that the whole of his later work was based on this long stressful period of his life.

Likewise Ignatius of Loyola, founder of the Society of Jesus, experienced deep depression that lasted for months. He evidently was temporarily manic-depressive and was subject to extreme alternations of mood. These times of depression in solitude constituted what he called his 'dark nights of the soul'. During them he felt alienated from God and was recurrently tempted to suicide. Storr borrowed the term 'creative illness' from Henry Ellenberger, who described the after-effects as follows: 'The subject emerges from his ordeal with a permanent transformation in his personality and the conviction that he has discovered a great truth or new spiritual world' (Storr 1997 p. 161).

A lot of unhappy people who are aware of their own situation spend a lot of time and sometimes a lot of money to replace their negative spirit with a positive one. And these days there is no end of gurus and cults and sects that offer ways out of this dilemma. Bookshops are full of 'how to feel good' books on 'self-help'. Lots of people must be buying them, judging from any list of bestsellers in each week's *New York Times Book Review*. This gives point to the Chinese proverb: 'People in the West are always getting ready to live'.

My second proposition is that our own existence and experience of aliveness provides the clue to understanding the nature of life of other living creatures. After exploring the meaning of aliveness in human life I explore its meaning in non-humans from this human perspective. And in so doing discover that there are organisms of organisms. It is more appropriate to think of the complex organism as an organism of organisms.

Thirdly, since there is no known dividing line between living organisms and the so-called inanimate world I ask what could be the meaning of aliveness at the level of organisation below what we recognise as living organisms—that is to say in molecules, atoms, and the so-called fundamental particles. And here again the principles that constitute the universe are sought in ourselves. There are bugs that infest the idea of a radically mindless matter. Physics long ago abandoned the idea of inert matter totally discontinuous with life. The whole is somehow needed in the description of the parts. Mary Midgley (1992) says 'the whole notion of "brute stuff" in the universe [has] lately been subject to an increasing run of bad luck' (p. 40). Substance or stuff is being replaced by event or process as in the concept that elementary particles such as electrons seem to retain a relationship with one another, however widely separated in the universe.

We can even ask if there is anything like the subjective at the level of electrons and atoms? Indeed the discoverer of the electron, J. J. Thomson, himself said that to know an electron you would have to be one. This is the interesting proposition that you don't really know what an electron is unless you have a first-person understanding of it. But of course ours is a third-person approach. We are denied, except imaginatively, what it might be like to be an electron. This is largely veiled in mystery though not completely from imaginative insights.

The idea that physics needs to take into account the existence of feelings in ourselves is not just a crazy notion that physicists and others can scoff at. It has its followers in such notable contemporary physicists as Freeman Dyson, David Bohm and Henry P. Stapp. If mind grows out of matter it is our conception of matter which needs revision. Physics has gone through many transformations in its view of matter. One of the strangest, yet now widely accepted, is this concept that matter consists not of particles, there are no particles, but of processes. Suppose all processes were to stop, what would be left? The answer of modern physics is nothing, not even a cold corpse! 'The world is a strange place,' says Nagel (1986), 'and nothing but radical speculation gives us the hope of coming up with any candidate for the truth' (p. 10).

Matter is not what it seems. Bertrand Russell once said: 'Matter is a word for our ignorance'. The explanations of the physical sciences as we know them are necessary but not sufficient. This revision is not a new project for humanity. It is a view which was promoted by some philosophers such as Epicurus and Plato about the same time as the development of materialism in the ancient Greek world. Much later Giordano Bruno was burned at the stake in Rome for this and other heresies. All reality, he argued, was composed inseparably of the physical and the mental. The object of philosophy, he said, was to preserve mind in matter and matter in mind from the lowest to the highest levels. Another Italian of the same period with similar ideas was Faustus Socinus. A reformer who fled from Italy to Geneva, his views were too radical for the Swiss reformation. Geneva under Calvin was no safe place for heretics. After Calvin burned the heretic and biologist Servetus at the stake in 1553, Socinus fled to Transylvania for his own safety. To this day Socinian teachings survive in Transylvania in the Socinian church.

It is appropriate to refer to the lower entities, such as atoms and molecules, as organisms since they are presumed to have some degree of freedom, self-determination and responsiveness. They are not simply inert, vacuous, completely determined bits of matter. They have some iota of self-determination and freedom, however small. The element of novelty in their being is negligible, yet negligible is quite different from completely absent. To suppose that negligible is the same as zero is the zero fallacy (Hartshorne 1997).

The view of life which I am suggesting is heterodox. It is implied in what Whitehead meant when he anticipated that one day biology would take over physics. It would bring to physics an understanding that could only come from understanding living organisms. We come back to this proposition many times in subsequent chapters.

Fourthly, there are some objects such as computers, tables, solar systems and nebulae which are quite complex in their organisation but which exhibit no aliveness. This suggests that aliveness has to do with particular sorts of organisation and complexity and not all sorts of complex organisations of matter. In considering this proposition we need to take account of those who want to tell us that the world is a supra-organism and some would say that it is itself alive. There are writers in astronomy who tell us that the complexity and 'life history' of nebulae is so complex that we should call them alive. I shall argue that individual entities of existence from protons to people are in some sense alive but that the world, nebulae and the universe as a whole are not alive, even though their ultimate constituents, be they protons and electrons or quarks, may have some qualities of aliveness. We humans, along with lots of other entities, including all plants and animals, are in a special category in the universe in having aliveness. It is an experience to be a human being. It is also an experience to be a cat or an amoeba. It is not an experience to be a nebula or a computer, though it may be experience to the atoms and molecules that make up these objects. I give reasons for this proposition later on.

THE CRITERION OF LIFE

Human beings, cells, non-human beings atoms and molecules have some things in common. They have some degree of freedom and self-determination. They take account of their environment internally. They are events and not substances. At one end of this hierarchy we normally refer to the entities as living. But we don't normally refer to atoms as living. Where then is the dividing line between living and non-living? The paradox is that there is none. There is a transition.

The living organism is characterised by novelty in its experience. It does not consist of the same experience moment by moment, day after day forever. Its degree of freedom accounts for its degree of novelty of experience. The degree of novelty is a criterion of livingness. Experience at the human level is characterised by a richness and great novelty. But the element of novelty in the atom or molecule must be so negligible that it would not be meaningful to call them living occasions, though I later argue that is meaningful to refer to them as occasions of experience. An alternative way of saying this is that they have subjectivity as well as objectivity. To do that is to put feelings at centre stage. This is an idea which is central in the thinking of a few physicists such as H. P. Stapp (1993) who conceives of every physical event at the most fundamental level as having an experiential aspect which he calls the *feel* of the event. We have to extend our understanding of the nature of matter.

When Whitehead (1938 p.167) said, 'Life is the enjoyment of emotion, derived from the past and aimed at the future' he was referring not just to human life but to whatever is alive. Further, he said that 'the characteristics of life are absolute self-enjoyment, creative activity and aim' (p. 152). He was using the same terms for both human life and the life of other organisms. The terms of the statement emphasise experience, self-enjoyment in experience, the influence of the past and the anticipation of the future. Physicist Niels Bohr expressed a similar idea when, searching for 'an ever richer description of life', he characterised all life as based on past experience reacting to future stimuli (Bohr 1958 p. 100). These are radical ways of thinking in contrast to materialism. The differences between different levels of life are differences in degree, not differences in kind.

THE CRITERION OF HARMONY

But you may well ask: how can I make a choice between a completely materialistic worldview and one which puts the emphasis on the subjective elements of life? Scientists normally ask of any hypothesis: how testable is it? A strict meaning of testability is whether the proposition is in principle falsifiable, which means that after every attempt to prove the proposition false it still stands. Such testability may well apply to the special sciences when they deal with a narrow range of observations and when controls are possible. But the criterion of testability does not apply to the hugely broad areas of meta-science.

We can be guided by Whitehead's proposition that cosmologies are never merely true or false; they are more or less adequate to the full variety of experienced facts. They are tested by their self-consistency and their adequacy to illumine all known facts. This is the principle of harmony. We may best think of the scientist who looks at the big issues as one concerned with the search for harmony, for an ordered picture of the universe into which to fit the facts as one fits together the pieces of a jigsaw puzzle. In the revolution of science in the sixteenth and seventeenth centuries men came to hold certain things to be true without empirical evidence to completely substantiate their developing theories. The Copernican theory that the Earth revolved around the sun seemed blatantly contrary to empirical fact. Galileo wrote that 'all experiments practicable upon earth are insufficient measures for proving its mobility since they are indifferently adaptable to an earth in motion or at rest'. When he stood before the charges of the Vatican he made it clear that he had no proof of his heliocentric theory. And Kepler knew of no empirical proof, yet he followed the Copernican system. He accepted the Copernican system because it presented a more harmonious and less clumsy picture of the world than the Ptolemaic system that preceded it.

A NATURALISTIC PHILOSOPHY

'Speculative philosophy,' said Whitehead (1929a p. 3) 'is the endeavour to frame a coherent, logical, necessary system of general ideas in terms of which every element of our experience can be interpreted ... the philosophical scheme should be coherent, logical, and, in respect of its interpretation, applicable and adequate.' He then went on to explain his meaning of coherent, logical and applicable and (on p. 5) wrote: 'The true method of discovery is like the flight of an aeroplane. It starts from the ground of particular observations; it makes its flight in the thin air of imaginative generalisation; and it again lands for renewed observation rendered acute by rational interpretation'.

So it is with our interpretation of the meaning of life. It should be consistent with tested scientific theory and with the rest of experience. And it should be open to the consequence of further exploration and discovery. In short it should be naturalistic as opposed to super-naturalistic. Naturalism is to see the world as it is so that quarks and planets and experience can be regarded as real in the same way.

It is should be compatible with the assured results of scientific theories without embracing a worldview of materialism. It should include a humility that recognises that at this point in history we are not yet in possession of the understanding necessary to comprehend absolutely everything. When physicists talk about a theory of everything (TOE) they are not talking about everything at all but a theory that would reconcile the major theories of modern physics into one acceptable theory of physics. That has as yet eluded them. Naturalism includes assured theories of physics and goes beyond them. 'This broader naturalism,' says Griffin (1998), 'besides accommodating mathematical, logical, ethical and aesthetic experience, can do the same for distinctively religious experience' (p. 206). We have to think big.

2

RICHNESS OF EXPERIENCE IN HUMAN LIFE

Now the way into the profounder levels of life is not to be found by means of physical and psychological analysis but only by means of intuitive insight, of apprehension of the basis of one's own aliveness.

Paul Tillich (1956 p. 58)

In chapter one I discussed some of the big questions about life which the science of biology has hardly yet addressed. One is the feeling of being alive—aliveness. This chapter focuses on that particular aspect of human life which we call richness of experience.

In the past two decades dozens of investigators throughout the world have asked hundreds of thousands of representatively sampled people to reflect on what psychologists variously call 'subjective well-being', aliveness, sense of satisfaction or happiness. In pursuing this state of well-being, Myers and Diener (1996) came to some surprising conclusions. More Americans than one might guess say they are happy with life. In a University of Chicago survey three in ten Americans say they are very happy with life. Only one in ten chose the most negative description 'not too happy'. Compared with the depressed, happy people are less self-focused, less hostile and abusive and less susceptible to illness. They have high self-esteem. They typically feel in control of their lives in contrast to those who feel no such control, such as patients in nursing homes and severely impoverished people. They have some close personal relationships which they value.

Wealth turns out to be a poor predictor of happiness. Even very rich people are only slightly happier than the average American.

Although Americans in 1996 on the average earned twice as much in real terms as they did in 1957, the proportion saying that they are 'very happy' remains relatively constant. People who win the lottery are no happier the year after the event than they were before. Indeed, in most nations the correlation between income and happiness is negligible. Only in the poorest countries such as Bangladesh is income a good indicator of a sense of human well-being. The study of what constitutes human well-being and happiness could help us to know how to build a society that enhances human well-being. Yet we tend to put the emphasis on material well-being, which is only one of the components that matter, and even then only for the less materially well-off in the community.

Eckersley (1998a) gives data for Australia which suggests that the majority of Australians are happy with their lives—at least they say they are. In 1997 some 86 per cent of Australians said that they were very or somewhat satisfied with their life. Thirty-nine per cent said they were very satisfied. On the other hand many surveys in the past decade show that Australians are concerned about the state of Australian society. A national survey of 1200 people aged eighteen and over found that 52 per cent believed life in Australia was getting worse, with only 13 per cent believing that it was getting better. A quarter said it was getting a lot worse. Why the differences in different surveys? The wording of questions is crucial. Asking about personal states elicits a more positive response than asking about general conditions and prospects. People don't want to be seen as losers.

There is a special problem in quality of life among youth today in the Western world which seems to contrast with the findings of more general surveys. There have been worsening trends in psychosocial problems leading to depression, delinquency, drug abuse, youth suicide, crime and associated unemployment. The statistics are quite horrendous, especially for youth suicide. Richard Eckersley (1998a, 1999b) has for more than a decade followed worsening trends in Australia. In 1995–96, 21.5 per cent of children were living in poverty (up by 6 per cent from 1966). Youth unemployment in 1997 was 20 per cent (up 3.3 per cent from 1967). Opiate overdose deaths increased sixfold between 1979 and 1995. The suicide rate of males aged fifteen to nineteen was 13 per 100,000 in 1986 and 17 in 1996. The rates for males aged twenty to twenty-four was higher. Despite these figures the rise in male youth suicides peaked in 1988 and appears to have plateaued after trebling since the 1950s. One-fifth to one-third of young Australians experience psychological distress. In his latest analysis Eckersley says that the roots of the problems lie deep in the nature of modern Western society; its priorities and values and their impact on personal, social and spiritual relationships that are crucial for well-being. Eckersley (1998b) is more specific when he pinpoints what he thinks are some of the underlying causes:

- The emergence of a youth culture that isolates young people from adults and increases peer and media influences; increased tension between dependence and the need for autonomy because of high unemployment and the longer time spent in education and more breakdowns in romantic relationships.
- Increased inequality and unemployment and a lack of opportunities in mainstream society.
- Parental conflict, separation, abuse and neglect leading to the absence of a close trusting relationship with a caring dependable adult. For many the family is a haven, for others it is a bear pit in which all their bitterness, frustration and anger are unleashed.
- Western society's failure to provide an adequate cultural framework of values, hope, meaning, purpose and belonging, both socially and spiritually. Youth are not inspired by the visions of the future held up to them by society. They regard social institutions, especially governments, with growing cynicism and mistrust.

The moral of this sad story is that these deeper causes need to be addressed far more than has been the case in the past. People need a guiding story to their lives which gives them a set of coherent values and beliefs. I have usually been somewhat embarrassed when Americans ask, what is your story? But I think I now know the importance of their question. It points to the health and wellbeing of young people as a critical measure of a society for two reasons. In moral terms, how well a society cares for its weak and vulnerable is a measure of how civilised it is. In more pragmatic terms, a society that fails to cherish and care for its vulnerable fails. The churches try to promote these values under their somewhat archaic phrase: 'God's preferential option for the poor'. The poor in this case mean the deprived and oppressed.

Eckersley says the bad news is that the overall situation is worse than he (and others) realised a decade ago in his earlier report. This is glaringly true of illicit drug use. The good news is that some aspects of the situation may have stopped deteriorating, such as the better treatment of adolescent depression which may have helped to stabilise the suicide rate. Some initiatives seem to have worked.

WHAT IS RICHNESS OF EXPERIENCE?

Rather than equate the sense of human aliveness with happiness I suggest that the concept of richness of experience gets closer to the meaning of human aliveness, yet it includes the component happiness. We get an idea of what richness of experience means by recollecting peak experiences. We can relive them in memory. Psychologist Abraham Maslow (1971) questioned people about their peak experiences by asking them: 'What is the most ecstatic experience in your life? What is the most blissful, joyous, happiest moment in your whole life? How did the world look different then? How did you change if you did, for peak experiences often have consequences?' The range of such experiences was very diverse, from sexual to mystical experiences, with love and music high on the list. An individual might recall vividly the first encounter with classical music as a peak experience and how from that day music was pursued as something wonderful in life. McDaniel (1989) recognises two components of richness of experience. They are harmony and zest. Harmony is accord, congruity, a sense of oneness between our ideas and our experience. It is atunement with our environment which includes other people and much more. Zest is energetic vitality exemplified in feelings of creativity, enthusiasm and passion. Zest is experienced in physical activities as well as in mental and emotional wellbeing.

Abraham Maslow (1971) approached the study of human experience not through a study of neurotic or psychotic behaviour but through a study of those people whom he regarded as outstanding examples of human life and who he called self-actualising people. A self-actualising person exhibits self-acceptance and lack of defensiveness, is not burdened by crippling shame or overriding guilt, is simple and spontaneous. Such a person is focused outside of self, has a sense of mission and enjoys solitude to a greater degree than the average person. Such a person has a feeling for humanity, a sense of community. The self-actualising person is more capable of love and is ever ready to learn from others. Creativity is the most universal characteristic of all the self-actualising people Maslow studied. They are better able to find a balance between reason and emotion, between self-centred and other-oriented behaviour, between the sensual and the spiritual. The self-actualising person is able to recognise, accept and deal with his or her own weaknesses.

The concept of richness of experience is dependent upon the recognition of the existence of intrinsic worth in every human being. When we say that human beings have intrinsic value we mean that each person is of value *in oneself* and *for oneself* quite independent of any usefulness one might be to others, which latter is called one's instrumental value. Value *in oneself* means that a person feels that his or her life is of value to oneself, they know it as an urge to live. They want to live, for life is worthwhile. William James (see Griffin 1998

p. 178) asserted that the only intelligible notion of something in itself is that it should be something for itself. Value *for oneself* is the sense of having individual experiences within oneself that are richly valued. Each of these subjective experiences has value in itself. The self-actualising person not only feels that life is worth living but is aware of particular experiences that are of enormous value in themselves. These experiences are mental or psychical realities, as contrasted with material realities such as possessions.

Intrinsic value in humans is not just one value for all human beings but has a range of values that is measured in terms of richness of experience. The richness of experience of a new-born babe is less than that of a youth or a mature adult. So too, the intrinsic worth of a person in a deep unending coma is less than that of an energetic alive mature person. It is important to be aware of such differences. The analysis of human life is not helped at all by supposing that intrinsic worth is the same for all people in all places at all times. It is not. Our richness of experience depends upon our environment. For example, a society whose social policy is not directed toward the enrichment of experience of individuals can leave its people deprived. A society which makes the rich richer and the poor poorer is a bad society. The focus of attention in a society guided by economic rationalism (neo-classical economics) is not on the richness of experience of individual persons but on their possession and consumption of goods and services. Such a society values science and technology for the goods and services they provide. But the real value of science and technology—and this is a radical proposition in our society—is how much value they bring into our lived experience. Do they make us more alive persons? Do they contribute to the richness of experience of our lives? In so saying I am not just referring to the goods and services provided by science but as well to its cultural values such as freedom from superstition and magic and its contribution to a richer understanding of the world around us as well of ourselves.

As already mentioned, possession and consumption of goods are correlated with richness of experience in poor societies. There are basic necessities, such as a roof over one's head and food, without which life is likely to be unfulfilled. A lead article in *The Economist* by Daniel Litvin (1998) commences with the following quotation:

> The centralisation of population in great cities exercises of itself an unfavourable influence. All putrefying vegetable and animal matter give off gases decidedly injurious to health, and if these gases have no free way of escape, they inevitably poison the atmosphere. The poor are obliged to throw all offal and garbage, all dirty water, often all disgusting

drainage and excrement into the streets, being without other means of disposing them; they are thus compelled to infect the region of their own dwelling. (p. 3)

So wrote Friedrich Engels in 1844 about working-class life in nineteenth-century London. *The Economist* goes on to say that Engel's description of working-class life in nineteenth-century London is an uncannily accurate picture of slum life in developing countries at the end of the twentieth century. The article goes on, in the following pages, to substantiate this claim. There is no doubt that million of people today live in misery because their basic needs are not met. The first requirement, if their quality of life is to improve, is to have housing, food, clean water and a proper system for disposing of waste. The bad news is that each year some 900 million people suffer from diarrhoea or diseases spread by contaminated water. The good news is that since 1980 some 2 billion people in developing countries have gained access to better water and another 400 million have got better sanitation. The provision of clean water and sanitation has resulted in a reduction of schistosomiasis (a debilitating disease caused by a parasitic worm) by 73 per cent and diarrhoea by 22 per cent. The immediate task for developing countries is to attain a level of standard of living for the whole population that will enable them to have the necessities of a wholesome life.

But quality of life is not only a problem of developing countries. Rich countries have two problems. One is their pockets of poverty. Secondly, for those who are not poor, after a certain level of affluence their quality of life deteriorates. Governments usually take as their measure of progress the growth in the gross national product. It is now widely recognised that this is not an index of human wellbeing at all. The less known index of sustainable economic welfare (ISEW) does better as it takes into account, not only consumption but also the distribution of wealth, environmental health and other indications of human wellbeing. Whereas in the USA the GNP rose steadily between 1950 and 1990, the ISEW showed a rise in welfare per person of some 2 per cent between 1950 and 1976. But thereafter, and despite a rising GNP, it fell by over 12 per cent by 1988 (Brown 1991 p. 10). The ISEW has been estimated for about half a dozen developed nations. All show a similar trend over the past fifty years, with ISEW increasing with GNP up to the 1970s, then levelling off or falling away while GNP continues to climb

A similar trend occurred in Australia, where an index similar to the ISEW has been calculated. This index is called the genuine progress indicator (GPI) and it incorporates over twenty factors that influence human wellbeing. In Australia between 1950 and 1966 GNP per person increased almost threefold. This suggests that Australians had become progressively much better off. However, the GPI index reveals quite a different picture. From 1950 to 1966 GPI rose by only about 1.8 times. And from 1970 to 1996 GPI showed no increase at all whereas GNP increased over this period (Hamilton & Saddler 1997). Yet increased GNP and economic growth are still the aims of most Western governments. In 1998 the prime minister of Australia clearly set the rate of economic growth as the prime benchmark by which to judge his government (Eckersley 1998b p. 8). This rationale for economic growth as we pursue it today is flawed in four important respects. Eckersley identifies these as: First, it over-estimates the extent to which past improvements in wellbeing are attributable to growth. Second, it reflects too narrow a view of human wellbeing and fails to explain why, after fifty years of rapid growth, so many people today appear to believe life is getting worse. The belief that material progress equates with a better life is so ingrained in our culture we are overlooking the importance of other factors—in particular, the personal, social and spiritual relationships that give our lives a moral texture and a sense of meaning, of self-worth, belonging, identity and purpose. Third, it underestimates the gulf between the magnitude of the environmental challenges we face and the scale of our responses to them. Fourth, it neglects the social costs of growing inequality

In the 1920s economist John Maynard Keynes looked forward to a time of abundance which would assure a decent level of consumption for everyone. He predicted the day is not far off when economic problems would take the back seat where they belong, and the head and heart would be occupied by real problems which he referred to as human relationships and religion. We haven't got there yet!

Keynes' forecast was wrong because he thought people would prefer more free time for the real issues of life than to spend more and more time accumulating material wealth. Why do people who already have a high standard of living continue to devote their lives to accumulating yet more wealth and goods? There is a Latin aphorism which describes them: 'For the sake of livelihood to lose what makes life worth living' (Livingstone 1944 p. 22). A reporter is reputed to have asked John D. Rockefeller: 'How much money is enough?' Rockefeller replied: 'A little bit more!' It is said of Samuel Goldwyn of Metro-Goldwyn-Mayer, when reminded that he can't take his wealth with him when he dies, replied, 'In that case I won't go.'

In each moment we tend to absolutise the good we have achieved and thus obstruct the growth of 'goods' of a different sort which we cannot foresee or understand. Achievements of the past can block, rather than foster, the development of a new, more desirable and more intangible sort of good. There is a word which describes this state. It is 'addiction'. Peter Singer (1993) has written a book on why people make the choices of lifestyle they do. He points out that most of the choices we make in our everyday lives are restricted ones, in that they are made from within a given framework or set of values. The rich man knows how to be rich and that is the framework of his choices in the future. He knows, or thinks he knows, what is of value to him and he continues to choose in that direction, even when it brings a sense of emptiness. He chooses the soft option. And there is the man who wanted to be rich so that he could despise money as he ought! Singer (p. 11) quotes Donald Trump from his book, *Surviving at the Top*, written at the height of Trump's massive wealth:

> It is a rare person who can achieve a major goal in life and not almost immediately start feeling sad, and empty, and a little lost. If you look at the record—which in this case means newspapers, magazines, and TV news—you'll see that an awful lot of people who achieve success, from Elvis Presley to Ivan Boesky, lose their direction or their ethics. Actually, I don't have to look at anyone else's life to know that's true. I'm as susceptible to that pitfall as anyone else.

A study was made in the USA comparing people with two sorts of beliefs. One group believed that happiness lay in the pursuit of external goals of wealth, fame and physical attractiveness. The other believed that happiness lay in the pursuit of intrinsic goals of personal relationships and contributing to the community. Which group were happiest? Answer: those with intrinsic goals. Furthermore, extrinsic-oriented individuals had shorter, more conflictual and competitive relationships that made a negative impact on the life of others. In short, the pursuit of goals for money and fame led to a lower quality of life than the goals of relatedness and community feeling (Eckersley 1999).

Concerning goals in life, there is an ancient Greek view alluded to five times by no less an authority than Plato. 'First comes health, second personal beauty, then wealth honestly come by, fourthly to be young with one's friends' (Livingstone 1915). Two items are very specific to the Greek aspiration: beauty of the body and youthfulness. The Greeks thought it a great misfortune to be ugly. They had an abiding passion for personal beauty. Plato thought physical beauty was the natural expression of beauty of the soul. So too they had a passion for being young and athletic with lots of young vigorous friends who shared the pleasure of being able to eat and drink and make love and run and play in dances, shows and processions. They loved the joyous *bon vivant*. When youth wore away, what made life worth living was gone. Old age had for them terrors which we do not feel so much. They were without spectacles, or hearing aids or a supermarket of medicines, or hip replacements and kidney transplants. But most of all they grieved the loss of capacity for youthful activity and enjoyment.

Sir Richard Livingstone asked his philosophy class in Oxford to write down four wishes in life in order of preference. Most put health first. Then close up came spiritual or moral excellence. After that, friendship or domestic happiness, then intellectual excellence. Contentment came next. Physical excellence and success were quite low on the list. Contrasted with the Greek point of view was their comparative indifference to wealth and physical excellence (Livingstone 1915 p. 126). That was a long time ago.

Recently I asked senior students in a leading private school in Sydney to write down for me what they found fulfilling in life. Here are some responses: 'I am not going to deny that what I want is money'; 'My mother has always stressed happiness as the most important thing and then some money on the side to buy that chateau in France'; 'I'm no goody-two-shoes who will spend the rest of my life in a monastery'; 'I'm like any other guy—what you've got to recognise is the urge at school to look cool and to fit in'; 'The idea of meaning to life takes a back seat to the scramble for money, exam results, a new house and car, wife etc'; 'After these comes the mid-life crisis'. But there were some other responses: 'I want to make a difference, to make a mark, at least a scratch'; 'Am I really noble enough to follow the truth?'; 'Intelligence is a chaotic force and we are inclined more to evil than to good'. Some of the students appeared to be indifferent: 'My mother said to me if you don't go to school what would you do?'; 'And as to goals, the simple fact is that I've got none'. What struck me with the responses was the extent to which conventional, materialistic values predominated. I was led to ask myself what difference does the family make, and also the school? My answer is: probably a lot. Certain family values become reinforced by the private school. These Sydney schoolboys had little resemblance to the Greeks and not much to Livingstone's philosophy students. Chasms separated each from the other.

Some ninety-seven second- and third-year students in a management course in a university in Sydney in 1998 were asked to list in order of preference what they wanted most in life (David Paul, personal communication). There was a total of twenty such wants. Unsurprisingly, at the top of the list was money and in particular inherited wealth. Second was long-term security. Fourth was sex, purely for pleasure without attachments and demands. They were not interested in obligations, love or morality or long-term commitment in their evaluation of sex. In between (third) was something less hedonistic: to change the way I feel and view myself, to live without worry of what others think of me and the desire to look more attractive and to 'ooze sensuality'. What others think of these young people is more important than how they view themselves. You don't ask what you think is cool but what you think others think is cool. They are deeply influenced by their peers. Fifth was to have a mentor, a role model—someone who is better than a parent and helps you face mistakes 'without thinking you are a fuckwit'. Parents and teachers are not 'cool' role models. Their views are not seen as important enough to shape their thinking or shape their perspectives. They are searching for someone they can emulate to shape them into better human beings. A mentor encourages rather than disciplines, guides rather than instructs, is a friend who motivates rather than one who is a moral advocate. A mentor believes in you rather that criticises you. Friends rank higher than *de facto* partners or spouses. Marriage was at the bottom of the list. Friends stick by you no matter what, while others walk out when the going gets tough.

These tertiary students give the strong impression that a materialistic lifestyle is high on their list. They want luxury items: a computer with a 300 MHz chip with a 4 gigabyte HD and 120 Mb of RAM or that fast car or an overseas holiday. Money makes such things possible. Yet there is a certain void in life that seeks to be filled. Relationships are not high on the list, sex is. Religion or a church do not even rate. A spiritual journey of discovery is halfway down the list, long after self-esteem and the desire for a mentor.

In contrast to the school students I questioned, these tertiary students did not get their values primarily from school or parents but from their peers, the media and the entertainment industry. Self-interest was to the fore. Selflessness was way behind.

Peter Singer (1993) makes a distinction between the sorts of choices of such as these tertiary students and what he calls ultimate choices. In an ultimate choice the fundamental values themselves come to the fore. We no longer choose within the old framework that assumes we want to maximise our own interests. Instead, we choose a different way of living in which ethics is paramount. Self-interest takes a back seat and the welfare of others becomes important. Ultimate choices take courage because they put in question the foundations of our lives. The excessively rich man continues to do what makes him richer because to do anything else would involve him in questioning the foundations of his life. The original route of his life seemed to him to be self-fulfilling. However, the will to self-fulfilment readily becomes transmuted into the 'will to power' (Nietzsche) and the desire for glory. When overweening self-interest becomes transmuted into the will to power it is ultimately destructive. It takes courage and insight to change from that track. In *The Republic* Plato traced the source of public tyranny in the state to lawless passion within the individual. It was the most gifted citizens who, because of their great possessions, were most tempted to fall victims to the lust for power and to shatter, first their own souls and then that of the community.

Many of Hitler's henchmen were quite ordinary people who lacked self-esteem until they found a purpose in the Nazi movement, and with that there came a lust for power. For some their overriding strategy was to please the Fuhrer, to be in his good books no matter what the cost in terms of humane values. Eichmann set his mind to eliminating Jews. Speer found his purpose in serving Hitler's architectural excesses. The reward was power. The cost to Speer in humane values was a mind closed to the terrible atrocities going on around him. He didn't see what was going on in the extermination camps but he must have known about it. Eichmann was witness to atrocities day after day. The cost to him was an anaesthetising of his mind to what he experienced.

The dividing line between the ordinary person without strong ambitions and the criminal can be a thin one. Timothy Garton Ash, renowned for his reporting of the cold war from Central Europe, spent some years studying Berliners during both the Nazi period and East Berliners under the German Democratic Republic. Concerning the latter, he found it quite impossible to distinguish the people who chose to work for the hated secret police (STASI) from those who chose the less financially rewarding jobs of teachers, social workers, artists or journalists. He got to know both. Some of his friends in the latter category told him that back in the late 1960s and 1970s they might have become terrorists. Members of the former STASI, whom Garton Ash interviewed, justified their work on the grounds that it contributed to security of the state (Garton Ash 1997).

It is easy to live unreflectively, without asking what our goals are. There are many reasons for this, some of which I have already suggested: addiction to the present, fear of the unknown, the drive to be immortalised in some major achievement, and the lack of courage needed to question the foundations of our lives. That's the bad news. But there is good news also. People do change! The Buddha and Jesus turned their backs on the conventional life whose values framed the societies they lived in. They chose quite other values that led to a revolutionary lifestyle. So did Raoul Wallenberg who gave his life to save thousands of Jews from Nazi terror in Hungary and Oskar Schindler, also a businessman, who saved countless Jews from being deported from his factory in Cracow to extermination camps. And there are Elie Wiesel, Primo Levi and Viktor Frankl whose spirits rose above the horrors of Auschwitz concentration camp to extraordinary heights that saved the spirits of countless others. As I write this thirty young Australians are receiving awards from the governor-general for acts of great bravery in the past year. Many more go uncited.

There is today a permanent exhibition in Berlin entitled Topography of Terror. It is on the flattened site of the former Gestapo headquarters on Prinz Albrecht Strasse. By means mostly of photographs from the Nazi period, it depicts not only the perpetrators of terror but more especially those, such as Dietrich Bonhoeffer, who struggled against these horrors. The price he and others paid was death in a concentration camp. Yet Bonhoeffer was able to write from prison about 'eternity in time, of life in death, of love in hate, of forgiveness in sin, of salvation in suffering, of hope in despair.' And there are the unsung heroes of every generation. The Peace Corps and the Australian equivalent, Volunteers Abroad, appeal to many young people who have become imbued with a sense of service to those less fortunate than themselves.

Peter Singer (1993) suggests that any one of us can become part of the critical mass that offers a chance of improving the world before it is too late. We can be part of the answer instead of being part of the problem. There is wrong side and a right side. To alter one word of the first line of an old hymn we can ask ourselves: who is on the right side? It is appropriately sung to the tune Armageddon! Everything in the long run depends upon enough people (not all of the people) who are part of the answer. And that depends not only on recognising the problem but on changing ourselves.

There is an extraordinary story in First Samuel where we read in chapter 28: 'Now Saul had cleared the witches and wizards out of the country'. Witch was the name given to necromancers who predicted by communication with the dead. Saul the king of Israel recognised witchcraft as a public evil and had issued an edict against it: all witches and wizards begone! Four verses later we read: 'Saul said to his courtiers, find me a witch that I may go and consult her'. Here is a man who recognised a public evil, but when the pinch came he became himself part of the problem. This is one of the most human passages in the Bible. All witches begone! But four verses later, Seek me a witch! And there is the anti-pornographer—pornography be gone—who reads a lot of pornography to make sure of what is not good for other people!

President Richard Nixon in his inaugural address said: 'all our problems are spiritual and must, therefore, have a spiritual solution'. In furtherance of this proposition he had Sunday morning services in the East Room at the White House to which he invited clerics such as Billy Graham to preach. Mr Nixon said he had established these services to further the cause of religion with particular regard to the youth of the nation (Niebuhr 1969). And all the time the president was involved in criminal activities that eventually resulted in his resignation before he would have been impeached. Reinhold Niebuhr (1969) contrasts these religious services (which could be seen as invoking religion to support Nixon's political policy) with the favourite text of Martin Luther King: 'But let justice roll down like waters, and righteousness like an everflowing stream' (Amos 5:24). He used it in his 'I Have a Dream' speech to thousands at the march on Washington which was a major step toward liberation for blacks. Further Niebuhr gives us the context: the prophet Amos addresses the king: 'I hate, I despise your feasts, and I take no delight in your solemn assemblies ... Take away from me the noise of your songs; the melody of your harps. I will not listen' (Amos 5:21,23). What a judgment on the head of state!

How do we become part of the world's answer? Think back for a moment to the critical mass of enlightened people who created civilisation as we know it in the Western world. Five hundred years before Christ a strange new power was at work in the small city of Athens. It was a time when the mighty civilisations of the ancient world had perished and the shadow of barbarism was dark over the Earth. In that shadowy world a little centre of white-hot spiritual energy was at work. A new civilisation had arisen in Athens unlike all that had gone before. What was then achieved in thought and art has probably never been surpassed. It so moulded the mind and spirit that our mind and spirit today are different, though it only survived in Athens for a couple of hundred years.

Sir Richard Livingstone (1935 p. 73) sees Hellenism as having four cardinal features. First, it had a power to draw men away from lesser aims to follow more ultimate causes. Second, it developed from lower to higher conceptions of the good in a vision that grew as human experience grew. Third, it led to a broad richness of experience in contrast to the provincialism of other systems. Fourth is the disinterestedness of its ideals, leading men to desire the good for itself and not simply for personal advantage. It drove them on from the lesser ideals of money, position and power to be the best of which human nature is possible. In addition to having these ideals of what life should be, the Greeks were promoters of science as finding rational explanations of the universe as exemplified in the work of Archimedes, Aristarchus Democritus and Hippocrates. The first Greek scientists were born into a world which believed that the sun and moon were gods and that thunder was produced by Zeus. They had a passion to know, a belief in reason. There was another quality which could be a fifth feature of Greek though. It was a modesty about the extent of their knowledge of anything. In their modesty they considered no system of thought as final. Human knowledge is relative and fallible and must be constantly revised in the light of further evidence. Socrates measured his advance towards wisdom by his growing consciousness of ignorance.

Above all was the noblest of all investigations—the study of what a man should be and should pursue. And this the Greeks did, despite their rather shambolic politics and the tragedy of everyday that wrecked so many lives. Socrates believed that goodness and truth were fundamental realities waiting to be discovered and experienced. They were attainable and every man would strive to attain them if he could be shown them. Socrates believed that his own mission was to open men's eyes to their ignorance and to lead them to where they could catch a glimpse of eternal truth and goodness beneath life's confusions and futilities. Each one must seek and find for himself. He was himself always the seeker and led others who came to him to seek. They discovered for themselves as the master led them from question to question. Socrates told them they discover for themselves not from him. The result was at first perplexity, sometimes extreme distress. Alcibiades told the company at a dinner table:

> I have heard Pericles and other great orators, but they never stirred my soul or made me angry at living in a way that was no better than a slave. But this man has brought me to such a pass that I felt I could hardly endure the life I was leading neglecting the needs of my soul. (Hamilton 1952 p. 167)

Socrates' own life did as much to arouse discontent as his words did. When he was taken to court on a life and death charge of corrupting young men by his teaching he refused to save his life by promising to give up teaching. In Plato's dialogue the *Phaedo* we are told that he ended by comforting his judges for condemning him to death. He told them to be of good cheer and know of a certainty that no evil can happen to a good man either in life or in death. In the prison cell when the time had come to drink the hemlock he had a kind word for the jailer who brought him the cup, breaking off the discourse with his friends about how beauty and goodness have a most real and actual existence. He exemplified in himself the excellence of the Greek vision.

Was the Greek vision of the good life too good to last? It became contaminated in a number of ways. Through Alexander's conquest the Hellenistic world extended all the way from the western Mediterranean to central Asia where it was exposed to a huge multiplicity of views. Thirty years of war drained much of the life out of the city state. Then with the eventual Roman hegemony the original cast of Greek thought did not hold. Nevertheless the achievement of a hundred or so years of a richness of life the world had hardly known before cast its brilliant light on the life of the Western world in the millennia that followed. Plato's Academy in Athens had a long and memorable history. It served as a model for Aristotle's college in the Lyceum. Athens continued as the central home of Platonic teaching for a thousand years.

Richness of experience has reached high peaks in human society. In the middle of the first millennium before Christ, apparently quite independently, spiritual leaders arose, not only in Greece, as we have just discussed, but also in China, India, Persia and Israel. These became the great movements of Hellenism, Zoroastrianism, Janaism, Buddhism, Confucianism, Taoism, Hinduism and Judaism with its later offshoots in Christianity and Islam. In each of these developments there were gains and losses. Christianity began as a zealous movement of the followers of Jesus to transform the world. To a large extent that it did, and with amazing speed. The spirit of Jesus' life passed into the lives of his immediate followers. Through them it passed into the world, transforming hearts and minds with a suddenness and swiftness without parallel. A new power was at work which revolutionised the entire fabric of the Mediterranean civilisation. It began with one man and a dozen followers. It lost something when it became the official religion of the Roman empire. Under the behest of Emperor Constantine the Council of Nicaea was summoned in 325 CE to settle disputes in the church about its doctrines. The emperor wanted a set of beliefs to be agreed by all. He got the Nicene Creed. Although still recited in churches it was itself the source of much further disputation in successive councils. Nevertheless, in each generation since those beginnings there are those who have sought to find again the water of life from which Jesus drew. It is well to remember that Christianity and Hellenism have been the only source of values in Western civilisation. If those two influences wane, from whence shall we derive out values in the future—nay even now?

THE CORRELATES OF RICHNESS OF EXPERIENCE

The richness of experience that these various world movements gave to their followers had certain elements in common. They apply to our experiences, no matter from what sources we draw. In what follows I have drawn heavily on a discussion in Birch and Cobb (1981 chapter 9).

RICHNESS OF EXPERIENCE IS DEPENDENT UPON RELATIONALITY

Individuals are constituted by their relations. Individuals exist in community and are constituted by the community in which they live. Life is process. This was exemplified in the Greek city-state where people knew each other and met in the marketplace and the Academy to discuss what life was all about—only connect! It was quite extraordinary how the thoughts of great thinkers of the day seemed to filter down to the populace. And there were many such thinkers. What mattered was the quality of life of the citizens.

A major criticism of traditional economics in our day is that it sees the individual as primarily a producer and consumer of goods and services. In its modern expression, it leads to dominance by the markets with community services and quality of life taking a secondary place. Its inadequacies and inequities have led to the formulation of possible alternative economic systems with an emphasis on community wellbeing. Hence the title of Daly and Cobb's (1990) book on this subject, *For the Common Good*. These authors argue against the dominance of the market and against free trade and for maximally self-sufficient national economies because at present free trade destroys existing national and sub-national communities in the name of a vaunted but mythical 'world community'.

A formative influence in the life of Tony Blair, prime minister of Great Britain, was the thought of the philosopher John Macmurray. Macmurray stressed the centrality of community. People are not individuals first who then choose to relate to others. People exist only in relation to others. They yearn in their lives to be connected. A society which is structured to allow this makes for a richer experience for the individuals in that society. In East Germany under communist rule people were greatly despondent at being cut off from friends in West Germany, let alone those on other parts of the world. On the other hand, oppression brought them together in a way less evident in the richer west. I asked a group of East Germans, in the village of Joachimsthal on the eastern outskirts of Berlin, what they liked most about living in a socialist state. One woman immediately replied—security. I asked her what she liked least about living in a socialist state and she replied—security! She appreciated the constant surveillance that meant she felt safe from crime but she detested the walls with which the state surrounded her life. The sort of society we live in does matter.

The noblest form of relationality is friendship. We should foster a sense of community in our society where people are committed to the wellbeing of one another. It is the antithesis of the individualist proposition of former prime minister Margaret Thatcher who will go down in history as the political leader who didn't know this truth. She claimed there was no such thing as society, there are only individuals. She seemed not know that individuals are what they are by virtue of the sort of society in which they live.

RICHNESS OF EXPERIENCE IS DEPENDENT UPON A TRANSCENDENCE OF PERSONS AND THINGS TO WHICH THEY ARE RELATED

No-one is merely a product of relationships in community. Each one of us creates a synthesis from our relationships that makes it possible for us to sustain a sense of wellbeing even when valued relationships disappear. 'It is good that I go away,' said Jesus to his disciples. It was as though he was saying to them: you are not to be dependent upon me, but you are to discover your own life's fulfilment in relation to the possibilities that are now yours. Any good teacher does the same with his or her students. No-one has to think and act just the way they were taught to think and act. The meaning of transcendence is that in any moment there is the possibility of creative novelty. Each new moment is an opportunity to learn from others and to be of service to others. Some people do care and feel that the need of another human being lays a claim upon them which is independent of private desires and social customs.

The notion of transcendence implies two things. First, it implies we are free to some extent to choose our own future. Life in its essence is the gain of intensity of experience through freedom. Secondly, it implies that there is a source of values and experiences from which we can choose to draw, call that source God or what you will. A great discovery of Plato was his recognition of an agency in the world, which he called divine, which is to be conceived as a persuasive agency and not coercive. We don't create the source of values. We appropriate it. The implication is that this source cannot dry up. It is not like a tank that can be emptied. It is more like a well fed by a ceaseless spring. Such is the nature of experience in our relationship to transcendence. Friendship leads us to the well. We discover a bottomless resource.

RICHNESS OF EXPERIENCE IS DEPENDENT UPON A REALISTIC ASSESSMENT OF POSSIBILITIES AT THE TIME

Each one of us is conditioned by our inheritance and our environment. To some extent this restricts the possibilities of the present moment. We are constrained by circumstance. We do not have an unconditioned perspective of life. There are many reasons for this. Charles Darwin had a passion to interpret nature. For a long time his thinking was limited by a theology which saw nature as totally determined by an all-powerful God. He had to snap out of this to begin to find an understanding that transformed the way he thought about nature and for that matter how he thought about God. As a scientist I may have a passionate interest in understanding the world around me but I am largely conditioned by interpretations that have gone before, particularly by what is now called Newtonian science. This perspective is now known, in the light of the new physics, to have limited applicability. It is still important but it does not have the comprehensive importance it was at one time thought to have.

Scientists and philosophers and, for that matter, the rest of us are subject to fashion and bias. The deconstructive postmodernism of Jacques Lacan, Jacques Derrida, Michel Foucault and their disciples is one such fashion. Its antirationalism asserts that we can never escape our cultural and historical biases and therefore all we can ever perceive about the world are shadows. It is nihilism in modern dress, trapped in its own verbal formulas. It has been described as 'a state of faddish delusion about life, art and thought' (Paglia 1991 p. 29). The deconstructive postmodernists claim to be playing games. Anything goes. There is no absolute truth. Anything written has the same status as anything else. They rewrite the ancient text to read: 'In the beginning was, not the Word, but the Situation'. It is a disastrous creed. For a full exposé read Sokal and Bricmont (1998), *Intellectual Impostures*. The good news is that with a critical mind we have some degree of freedom to escape the embrace of deconstructive postmodernism. The possibilities open to each of us at any time depend on how we resolve central tensions in life.

There is another sort of repressive fad today. It is genetic determinism or sociobiology, which has recently changed its name to evolutionary psychology. This asserts that we cannot escape the genetic bias with which we were endowed at birth. A lot about us is dependent upon our genes, but not all that the genetic determinists claim. They claim that how we are brought up and the nature of our family background play a lesser role than genes. Newspaper and magazine articles bring us news of the latest supposed discovery of genes responsible for IQ, schizophrenia, alcoholism, criminality, cancer, homosexuality and much more. With genetic determinism comes the belief that interventions by social workers cannot solve these problems. This is a debate that has taken place in every generation since Darwin's day. But, I ask, is present day genetic determinism good science? There are a number of facts and arguments indicating that it is not. As for character—it is not born but made. A detailed case against genetic determinism is well put by Lewontin (1991) and Rose (1998) and is discussed in chapter 4.

RICHNESS OF EXPERIENCE IS DEPENDENT UPON THE CONTINUITY BETWEEN HUMAN BEINGS AND THE REST OF THE NATURAL WORLD

No-one is an island to himself or herself. We are dependent not only upon other persons but also upon the rest of the natural world. The relations that constitute us are not only relations with other human beings. We are impoverished by the decay of the non-human environment which includes species that become extinct day by day as a result of our activities on the Earth. Biophilia is a term invented to give a name to the natural ties we seem to have with the natural world around us. We need more than bricks and concrete in our environment. Humanity can neither be understood nor saved alone.

RELATIONSHIPS WHICH PEOPLE RECOGNISE AS IMPORTANT

Josselson (1996) interviewed sixty people of ages from eleven to ninety-three to find out what relationships they felt were important in their lives. She identified eight primary ways in which people relate in a way that is meaningful to them.

- Holding represents security and basic trust. Someone is there for you. Powerful arms prevent the child from falling.
- Attachment: the infant has attachments to its mother who provides succour and support. Throughout life we continue to form attachments that help us to feel secure. It is very important for adolescents as they face new stresses to have loving parents or a mentor to whom they respond. The dark side is to lose such an attachment through death or parting in other ways such as becoming a refugee or other victim of war. There is also a primary attachment to nature (biophilia, referred to above).
- Passionate experience is exhibited in sexual union or symbolic ways of expressing this and as well in the intense pleasure found in a relationship to nature.
- Eye-to-eye relating: the other becomes a mirror to ourselves beginning for the infant with the mother and developing later into family relationships and to those beyond family which can include companion animals.
- Idealisation and identification with others, trying to be where they are and so expanding ourselves. We find role models, mentors and a sense of place.

- Mutuality: companionship in which there emerges a bond in the relationship such that we resonate with the other.
- Embeddedness: we feel like the bit of the jigsaw that fits into the picture. It is finding a place in which we feel at home and to which we belong . The immigrant from Europe to the New World finds himself or herself in a town and country in which all is strange. For them to eventually discover a sense of place is extremely important.
- Tending and caring for others, first cradling them in our arms and later becoming a person who feels for others, particularly in time of need.

The Buddha spoke of four fulfilling states described as loving kindness, compassion, sympathetic joy and equanimity. Each of these states is a mark of the opening of the heart. Yet each has what he called a near enemy that mimics the true state (Kornfield 1988).

- Attachment is the near enemy of loving-kindness. In the meaning of the Buddha, attachment is characterised by clinging. It may feel like love but it grows into the opposite. All life, says the Buddha, is suffering. We suffer because we are attached to things. When we relinquish this attachment, when we cease to cling, we become free. Christianity also teaches that attachment to the world leads to suffering. Salvation involves overcoming our craving for worldly security, reputation, success and achievement. Cobb (1982 p. 78) considers that the Buddhist demand is more radical than anything found in the West. The Christian struggles against selfish interests so as to come to pure love of the neighbour. The Christian tries to free self from worldly attachments so as to devote the self more completely to spiritual goals. Commitment and love in the Christian sense ultimately bind one to suffering as tightly as do lust and greed. Not so in Buddhism, which seeks release from suffering. Because the Buddha can also so easily serve as an object of attachment, there is a famous Buddhist saying: 'If you meet the Buddha, kill him'. There is to be no bondage either to Christ or Buddha. The catchphrase of a modern and popular evangelical movement, 'Have a Crush on Christ', would be totally rejected by the Buddha and indeed by many Christians. In one sense Nirvana is the total absence of attachment, clinging or craving. Cobb points out that Christian teaching contains some similar paradoxes. Jesus warned that we find life only by giving it up.
- Comparison is the near enemy of both compassion and sympathetic joy (the joy in the happiness of others). Instead of rejoicing with

the other a subtle inner voice asks, is mine as good as yours? It looks to see if we have more of, the same as, or less than another. Indifference is the near enemy of equanimity. Equanimity is calmness of mind or composure, even in the midst of tantalising experience. Indifference is withdrawal and not caring. It is a running away from life. Equanimity is an acceptance of one's feelings. Indifference is a denial of one's feelings. Some historical analysts are now realising that the seeming equanimity of much of the population of Germany under Nazism was in fact indifference. Elie Wiesel survivor of concentration camps went to far as to say that:

> The opposite of love is not hatred
> The opposite of hope is not despair
> The opposite of mental health is not madness
> The opposite of remembering is not forgetting
> In every case the opposite in nothing but indifference.

Timothy Garton Ash (1997) spent much time in East Germany where he became an object for investigation by the STASI, the much hated secret police. After the demise of the German Democratic Republic he was able to get access to his STASI file and from there went on to investigate and interview those who informed and spied on him. What he found was less malice than human weakness, less deliberate dishonesty than an infinite capacity for self-deception. They were too easily shaped by circumstance. He did not use the word indifference but these people did become indifferent to humane values. Not one of them did he describe as evil. Yet the sum of their actions was a great evil. It staggers the mind to realise how much effort went into making the STASI files which fill sixty or more kilometres of shelves in Berlin. Some space is even taken up with a file on myself since I visited East Germany a number of times. It contains details of when I arrived, where I went, whom I met and the letters I wrote in preparation for my visits. Any visitor was suspect in that sort of society.

What is it that makes one person an informer and another a member of the underground resistance? Or as Garton Ask asks: 'What makes one person a Stauffenberg, another a Speer?' Stauffenberg was the German Army officer who attempted to assassinate Hitler and was himself executed soon after. Speer was Hitler's architect and war administrator who was condemned by the Nuremberg trial to twenty years in prison for war crimes. In answer to his question about the difference between a Stauffenberg and a Speer, Garton Ash says that twenty years on he is little closer to an answer.

QUALITY OF LIFE IN THE WORKPLACE

Every organisation that employs people, be it a university or a bank, needs to ask itself from time to time: what is our organisation for? A common answer of commercial organisations is: to make a profit for our shareholders. Some business leaders, when asked, go one step further and add to the profit motive the provision of a service to the community as a conscious purpose of their organisation. A bank sets out to make profits for its shareholders and at the same time provides a service to its customers. These are both legitimate goals. But they are not enough? Organisations consist of people who have chosen to spend much of their hours and days in the organisation working for it. So what about the quality of their lives within the organisation? Does that count?

Does the organisation help to fulfil the lives of its staff in addition to providing a salary? Or does it do the opposite when staff feel compelled, indeed are compelled, to work into the late hours, giving less time to their families and other pursuits? If change is to come it must come from the senior executives. What they do by arriving at 7 a.m. and leaving at 8 p.m. is to send a message: do this and you will also succeed. Furthermore, home itself becomes a place to bring back work from the office. Home becomes work. Or take the case of the chairman of the boards of a number of companies who had been flying to and from Sydney and Melbourne every night for a week or so, who had spent 355 hours in the air on international flights in three months, who also smoked seventy cigarettes a day and drank fourteen cups of coffee and never drank water. Overworked with a poor lifestyle, this senior executive paid the price in the form of a blood clot in the main vein that takes blood away from the brain. The proximate cause was said to be dehydration of blood brought about by too much air travel, smoking and coffee. The ultimate cause was poor quality of life in the workplace.

It is not so much that we need more leisure. Leisure in its current meaning is the wrong word as it suggests the time when you are not working and getting ready to do some more work. The original meaning of the Greek word for school is 'leisure'. School is the place where the Greeks' leisure hours were spent! Scientific research was a natural occupation of their leisure. In good work you don't know whether it is work or play. What matters is to enjoy what you are working at and see to it that you give time to the other pursuits that make for a good quality of life. That is the original meaning of leisure. I have worked in a number of universities in the USA. Each time I have been overwhelmed by the long hours in the laboratory by graduate students and their supervisors. About the only time they took off was to see their psychiatrist! Why did they work such long hours? They put far too much emphasis on the time spent than on what was achieved. By contrast, in my one experience in the UK, which was at Oxford, I found the graduate students and staff appeared well after 9 a.m., took time off for morning and afternoon tea and then high tea, with lots of time in between talking. I would estimate that each hour they spent in the lab was more productive than each hour of their American counterparts. I am glad to say that the Australian students I have known are more like those at Oxford than those in the USA.

According to a survey of 5000 workers made by the Australian Council of Trade Unions in the 1990s, about one in four Australians takes time off work each year for stress-related illnesses. Nearly seven in ten of those surveyed cited an increased workload as a factor that affected their performance in the office, and about one in five said overload of work was the most stressful circumstance in their workplace. Seven in ten cited organisational change and restructuring as a factor that affected their work, and one in ten said this was the most stressful aspect of their workplace (Powell 1997). People evidently find restructuring of the organisation very stressful and there has been a lot of that in the '90s. Restructuring of the organisation has meant that fewer people are responsible for more tasks and these take more time. The lower the level of job satisfaction and the greater the demands on time, the greater the likelihood that an employee will develop a stress-related illness.

If there is too much work to be done to fit into normal working hours, why doesn't the organisation employ more people? Why not cut back on overtime and long working hours and employ more people? Primarily because if productivity and profits are the prime goals, to get more out of less is seen to be better. But is it always better, even on these narrow criteria? Germany and France both chose to share work more equitably and have successfully created more jobs. They have cut hours, extended vacations, shortened the working week, given more holidays and sabbaticals for study and retraining. By contrast many workers in Japan fall prey to *karroshi* or 'death by overwork'. Ricardo Semler (1994) became head of an industrial concern in Brazil that had all the symptoms of a dissatisfied staff and unsatisfactory working conditions. He decided to 're-engineer' the organisation in a radical way. Critics said that his organisation would now be unprofitable. It wasn't. They said that staff don't want to be brought into discussions. They did. His is an example of reorganisation that humanised an industry and paid off all around.

A past government of South Australia, established a 'unit for quality of work-life' Its motto was: 'Make life work'. And that is just the point. You make life work if the main part of each day is fulfilling, adding to your enrichment of experience. Work becomes a real part of living. It is easy enough for me to say that when all my life I have been paid to do the things I enjoy, that is teaching and research in a university. At least in the past that has always been possible for a privileged few. But it never has meant that universities do not need to question their purposes and how they can be achieved. In my experience, every five to ten years these questions become critical again, for the ideal is never achieved for long, if at all.

The 1990s in capitalist countries, notably the USA, has been a time of exceptional economic growth, yet also of down-sizing, loss of jobs and change of one's profession which have had a profound effect on human lives. In the view of sociologist Richard Sennett (1998), the working conditions of modern capitalism are eating away at loyalty, commitment and the kind of long-term thinking that used to make even the most routine work a central ingredient in an orderly life. Sennett paints a bleak picture of what has happened to the downsized IBM executive and his colleagues. Yet he is not without hope. While he sees modern Americans denied the satisfactions of order and rootedness in the workplace, they are nevertheless beginning to rebuild their lives from scratch. He sees as an unintended consequence of modern capitalism that it has strengthened the value of place, aroused a longing for community and for some a scene of attachment and depth, perhaps most of all in family relationships.

A university periodically needs to ask itself what is its purpose. Its answer will necessarily be rather more complicated than that of a commercial organisation such as a bank. The university is a five-legged creature, those legs being scholarship, teaching, research, public affairs and innovation. If the staff are going to do these five jobs they are obviously not going to have much time to spend on any individual student. You may say, let's have some staff mainly concerned with teaching and others with research and innovation and so on. But that is not really good enough. The people the best students want to meet and participate with are not only the good teachers, but also the good innovators or researchers, or the people in contact with industry and government. A university that has a student–staff ratio of 20 to 1 or worse is not going to be able to satisfy these demands. The result will be declining quality of university life for students and staff. To halt the downhill slide, much innovation will be needed in teaching and in research facilities and the numbers of students per member of staff will need be improved.

A perennial problem for universities about life in the workplace is what to do with information that doubles every five years. More information was produced in the period of twenty-five years during which I was a professor than in the previous 5000 years. About one thousand books are published in the world every day. How does a university cope with this avalanche? Running out of information is not the problem, but drowning in it is.

One way in which drowning in information is overcome is by the discovery of principles and theories that tie up a lot of information previously untied. Prior to Charles Darwin biology was a mass of unrelated facts about nature. Darwin tied them together in a mere three principles of evolution: random genetic variation, struggle for existence and natural selection. So we do not need to teach every detail that was taught in the nineteenth century to students. A mere sample is enough to illustrate the universal principles. This problem of a university is a relatively easy one.

Much more challenging is the frontier where agreement on universals has not been reached. The Australian philosopher John Anderson urged his students not to ask of a social institution such as a university: what end or purpose does it serve? but rather: of what conflicts is it the scene? Its was Anderson's insight that it is through conflict and sometimes only through conflict that we learn what our ends and purposes are. A third problem for universities is the balance between teaching and research. The professors need to have enough teaching to stimulate and keep them human, not enough to distract them from the pursuit of knowledge in their research. Clark Kerr, a former president of the University of California, described the modern university as tending toward becoming the central manufacturing plant of the knowledge industry. He asked for improvement of teaching, unification of the intellectual world, humanisation of administration and a chance for all students who have genuine interest and capacity. He summarised by saying: 'The university may now and again need to find out whether it has a brain as well as a body' (Hutchins 1968 p. 121). The analogy is apt for the brain, though consisting of many compartments, each with a name, has myriad interconnections between these compartments as in no other organ of the body. Yet the increasing departmentalisation of universities, however necessary for administrative purposes, tends to trivialise the mentality of the teaching profession which then loses sight of what knowledge is for. There is hardly a nobler aim of education that that given by Saint Bernard of Clairvaux (1090–1153):

> To desire to know for the purpose of knowing is curiosity.
> To desire to know that you may be known is vanity.

To desire to know that you may sell your knowledge is mean trading.
To desire to know that you may be edified is prudence.
To desire to know that you may edify is love.

For commercial organisations such as banks and industries, the questions of purpose and work become even more critical because it is not as easy for all employees to find purpose in their work. And it is true of all sorts of organisations, be they banks or universities, that people with fulfilled lives contribute more to the organisation than those with frustrated lives.

In his bestseller, *The 7 Habits of Highly Effective People*, Stephen Covey (1989) puts an emphasis on personal qualities that tend to get second place in organisations. He deplores that so little is said of the personal needs and characteristics of people who work in organisations. He claims to try to get people to work on themselves and their relationships, then on the organisation. He thinks that the preponderance of mechanistic ways of talking about commerce has meant that managers fail to stay in touch with their humanness. It also seems likely that the dominance of the computer adds to the mechanisation of the workplace and the people who work in it. Michael Lawrence, head of the School of Information Systems at the University of New South Wales, says that his research 'shows a deep resistance by humans to having their lives taken over by the computer'. The computer is okay in its place, but let it stay there and not seek to look like or attempt to take over legitimate human functions' (Lawrence 1997 p. 48).

During World War I the number of British youths entering the army who received a fitness classification of C greatly disturbed the nation. Later returns from the forces showed that 90 per cent of recruits offering themselves were considered to be unfit. (Williamson & Pearse 1931). Williamson and Pearse identified obvious deficiencies such as poor nutrition. But an overall factor was the social environment of youths that included family home, friends and acquaintances, the district they live in and the work they did. These concerns led Williamson and Pearse to carry out a social experiment. In 1926 in the London borough of Peckham they established a club that was based on the whole family, not individual membership. An account of the now famous Peckham experiment is detailed in Kenneth Barlow's (1988) book, *Recognising Health* and in Pearse (1979).

The Peckham Centre had a special focus, namely the quality of life of the people who came to it. It saw health as more than the absence of disease. It was particularly concerned about how unsatisfactory human behaviour contributed to a poor quality of life. It saw the family as an untapped potential for harmonious living and creativity. But the environment had to be right. At the centre people began to make friends in a way that had been quite impossible in their homes, where overcrowding was such that any social life whatever was liable to lead to an invasion of the home. These initial moves were so successful than an expanded centre was set up in 1935, together with a group of doctors and social workers. An important aspect of this experiment in quality of life was the willingness of those in charge to let the members set the agenda. Really splendid facilities such as swimming pool, gymnasium, consulting rooms and cafeterias were provided.

At first it was thought that the best approach was the conventional one with instructors and timetables. But despite the involvement of members in the planning, that was a flop. Few participated. After much observation and thought it appeared that the problem was that instructors and timetables were too much like school. At the centre people came because they wanted to come and to be part of a community that was not regulated like home and school. The solution was to admit the members to various activities individually and let them get on at their own pace. The place became a hum of activity. It sounds simple but there was a lot of planning behind it. This was an experience of relevant order emerging out of lives previously in a state of chaos. It was self-organising activity resulting in developmental order. They had discovered Whitehead's (1929a) insight that 'The art of progress is to preserve order amid change and to preserve change amid order' (p. 339).

The result was a striking improvement in all-round health. Those in charge interpreted what was going on as a discovery of human potential within the individual, the family and the local community. When that potential is realised there is health.

The Peckham Centre has been compared with the Agora of ancient Athens where citizens met each day to discover what was important in their lives. The Agora was the principal square of ancient Athens and the centre of its public life. The Greeks were creators of science, philosophy, political thought and much else. They were the first people to ask rationally what is the right life for human beings. When Paul the Apostle went to Athens in 50–51 CE he 'discussed daily in the Agora with those whom he met' (Acts 17:17). Had he been a few hundred years earlier he might have talked with Socrates. Paul tells us that all the Athenians and foreigners he met spent their time doing nothing but talking about and listening to the latest ideas (Acts 17:21). Of the many altars in the Agora Paul noticed one dedicated 'To the Unknown God'. That was a cue for

Paul to tell the Athenians gathered there about the God he had discovered that transformed his life. He entered into the life of the community in the Agora. Before him Socrates had found this a fruitful place to discuss the issues of life that were paramount to him. We each need an Agora wherever we live so that we too create our community. It might be a church or some other 'community of faith' or a community centre or a village that sometimes springs up within a suburb of a big city.

There is much evidence that people who live in poor communities are much less healthy than those who live in affluent ones (Epstein 1998). We live in an age of rising income inequality and increasing health inequality. The causes of these differences are much debated. One much debated proposition is that inequality itself is a direct cause. It is the proposal that, for example, lower grade civil servants in Britain tend to come down with more serious health afflictions that those in grades above them. The risk of dying of heart attack was said to increase steadily right down the chain of command and this was due to stress being greater in the lower categories. If this is true it is surely a matter which should be of concern in any hierarchical organisation. One should choose to go up rather than to stay down!

Much less contentious is the proposition that quality of life is strongly related to the sense of community we experience in the society in which we spend our lives. Epstein (1998) draws attention to the fact that life expectancy in Britain increased by more than six years during the decades that included the two world wars. This was nearly twice as fast as during any other decade. This was the case even though thousands of soldiers died in battle, bombs wrecked much of London killing 30,000 civilians, and even though medical services were diverted to the troops and living standards fell. Epstein supports the proposal that the reason was that Britain became more egalitarian during the wars. The world wars were high points in British civil life. There was full employment and high taxes meant that the rich were poorer while the incomes of the poor increased. There was an ethos of cooperation and common striving. The nation for a time seemed to be of one mind. Healthy societies are those with a sense of community and common purpose. We need today a drive that William James called 'the moral equivalent of war'.

Another example which Epstein (1998) quotes as supporting this proposition is life in the small town of Roseto in Pennsylvania, which was settled by immigrants from southern Italy in the 1880s. During the 1950s doctors found that Roseto residents died of heart attacks at half the national rate. All sorts of medical experts descended on the town. They took details of the food people bought and how they prepared it. It was all pretty rich Italian fare. Furthermore they found that Rosetans smoked heavily and consumed vast amounts of fatty substances. The sociologist Stewart Wolf believed that the secret of Roseto's health lay in the quality of social life there. Social life was centred around the church and the extended family. Young people had plenty of leisure activities such as singing together and playing in brass bands. Adults joined the Holy Name Society and social clubs. At picnics factory owners mingled with their workers. There seemed to be no social divisions in Roseto. People lived in similar houses and ate much the same food. But in the 1970s life changed in Roseto. A new, more American generation of Rosetans came of age. Young people moved away. The well-to-do built larger houses. They bought Cadillacs, walled off their gardens and no longer invited their relatives to move in. By 1985 the rate of heart attack in Roseto had risen to the same level as in surrounding towns. Whereas the rate of heart attack in America overall was falling it failed to do so in Roseto. The only things that had changed, according to Wolf, who spent nearly fifty years studying the town, was the degree of cohesion in social life. Roseto had become a lonelier place. People did not seem to care any more about each other.

If we look at the world as a whole the quality of life is very grim because its resources are so unevenly distributed. Donella H. Meadows has a website entitled 'If the World were a Village of 1000 People'. In that village of today 200 people receive 75 per cent of the income, another 200 at the bottom of the scale receive only 2 per cent of the income. The village has a total budget per year of over $3 million—$3000 per person if it were distributed evenly, which is isn't. Only 70 people own an automobile though some of these own more than one. Of the total $3 million $181,000 goes to weapons of war, $159,000 goes to education and $132,000 goes to health care. About 300 have access to clean drinking water. Of the 670 adults in the village, half are illiterate. In each year ten people die, three of them from lack of food, one from cancer; two of the deaths are babies. One person of the 1000 in the village is infected with the HIV virus. The village has five soldiers, seven teachers and one doctor. Beneath the village is buried enough explosive power in nuclear weapons to blow itself into smithereens many times over. These weapons are under the control of just 100 people. The other 900 villagers are watching them with anxiety, wondering whether they can learn to get along together. And if they ever decide to dismantle the weapons they wonder where in the world village would they dispose of the dangerous radioactive materials of which the weapons are made. The village has 6000 acres in all, of which about 1900 acres are woodland and are desert, tundra, waste land and pavement. The woodland is rapidly declining and the desert wasteland category is expanding. This way of presenting the present word scenario makes it clear enough that the state of the world's quality of life is grim.

Quality of life depends upon many things as the various examples in this chapter illustrate. For those of us who are professionals or otherwise have a secure job it is not enough to live for our profession.

Tosca sings 'Vissi d'arte' (I lived for art) at the moment when she realises that yes, she did live for art, but art was not enough. Despite art's ministrations she had just betrayed a friend to political enemies. She now has to leave art behind to assassinate a tyrant. Her aria is a paean for art and yet of regret at its limitations, an expression of confusion about how unrelated moral action and art can be. This is a confusion that reached its nadir under Nazism. And so it can be in any profession which does not make life work. The focus of this chapter has been on examples of what constitutes richness of experience in human life and why it is important. In the next chapter I ask: to what extent does biology help us to understand this aspect of our lives that is so important?

3

IS LIFE REDUCIBLE TO PHYSICS AND CHEMISTRY?

A biology of parts becomes a medicine of spare parts and organisms become aggregates of genetic and molecular bits with which we can tinker as we please ... this is the path of ecological and social destruction.

Brian Goodwin (1994 p. 215)

We need scarcely add that the contemplation in natural science of a wider domain than the actual leads to a far better understanding of the actual.

Arthur Eddington (1928 p. 267)

We live at a time of 'nothing but' philosophies. Each of us is 'nothing but a pack of nerve cells' says the neurophysiologist. The human mind is 'nothing but a computer program' says the exponent of artificial intelligence. We are 'nothing but lumbering robots whose genes create us body and soul' says the geneticist. We are 'nothing but our genes' says the sociobiologist. A proposition of this book is that the answer is none of the above We may well ask the neurophysiologist, the artificial intelligencer, the geneticist and sociobiologist: but where is the human?

There is a story of a rabbi in a Viennese joke. There were two neighbours: one of them contended that the other's cat had stolen and eaten two kilos of his butter. There was a bitter argument and finally they agreed to seek the advice of the rabbi. They went to the rabbi and the owner of the cat said: 'It cannot be, my cat does not eat butter at all'. But the other insisted that it was his cat so the rabbi decided: 'Bring me the cat'. They brought him the cat and the rabbi said: 'Bring me the scales'. And they brought the scales and he asked. 'How many kilos of butter?' 'Two kilos.' And believe it or not, the weight of the cat was exactly two kilos. So the rabbi said: 'Now I have the butter, but where is the cat?' We may have all the physics and chemistry to do with the human—but where is the human person?

REDUCTIONISM

It would be true to say of all the 'nothing but' philosophies that their objective is to reduce life to physics and chemistry. Their model is the mechanistic model. It sees all aspects of the living in terms of a machine. This has become built into the whole of the Western way of looking at things, including the whole of our science. Or to put it another way: the nothing but-ers are reductionists. They break down the living organism into smallest bits and pieces, technically called substances, which are the classical physicist's so called fundamental particles, and from the bits they try to build up the organism. And what they get that way is, of course, a machine. Reductionists try to explain the properties of the complex wholes in terms of the units of which they are composed. There could hardly be a more reductionist statement than that of the eminent sociobiologist E. O. Wilson (1998) who, promoting the concept of consilience (the unity of knowledge), said:

> The central idea of the consilience world view is that all tangible phenomena, from the birth of stars to the workings of social institutions, are based on material processes that are ultimately reducible, however long and tortuous the sequences, to the laws of physics. (p. 266)

Such reductionism is to commit what Whitehead called 'the fallacy of misplaced concreteness' (1925 p. 64). The fallacy is to mistake abstractions for concrete realities. A living, thinking, loving human being is a concrete reality. The mechanist model of a human being which reduces the human to physics and chemistry is an abstraction. It is a perfectly valid analysis to make, but it should be recognised for what it is—namely an abstraction from the real world. There is more to be said about being alive. Mechanism is our *metier* or trade in science. At the same time it is our limitation. The fallacy of misplaced concreteness is a source of great confusion, not only in the scientific analysis of the human but also in economics, sociology and other fields of study of the human.

Even so, the reductionist program has led to most of the advances in science, including those in biology, from the foundation of biology in the renaissance of science in the sixteenth century to the latest discoveries in molecular biology. It works—at least for the sorts of problems it investigates. The great success of Galileo and Newton was based on a new mechanical model of the universe. They thought the universe was like a clock. But at least Newton did not make the mistake of saying it was a clock. That would have been to commit the fallacy of misplaced concreteness. William Harvey interpreted the workings of the heart in terms of a pump. And indeed it is like a pump, it has valves and chambers through which fluid is pumped. The job it has to do is to pump.

Yet the heart is unlike any mechanical pump in the way it is made and what it is made of. It is made of what Goodwin (1994 pp. 56–60) calls 'excitable media'. By this he means that the pumping action of the heart is dependent upon the relations that exist between the cells in the different parts of the heart that lead to ordered contractions. The individual cells respond to electrical messages coming to them from a set of cells called the pacemaker. The heart can function on its own without any external nerve supply, though there are major nerves that can adjust the pace depending upon what is happening in the rest of the body. I vividly recall seeing for the first time as a schoolboy a demonstration by the professor of physiology (there was only one in Melbourne then) of a heart severed from the body and happily beating away on its own while it was kept moist by drips of saline. This was my first and very exciting lesson of a 'self-exciting system'. What I want to get across is that while it is correct to say that the heart is like a pump or even is a pump and operates according to some of the hydraulic principles of a force pump, it is not in all its properties identical with a mechanical pump made by an engineer. To say it is identical is to commit the fallacy of misplaced concreteness. This living pump is not identical with a mechanical pump though it shares many of the same properties.

The mechanical metaphors we use to describe living systems are helpful, provided we say this or that living system is like this or that mechanism. At the time of the renaissance of science, due to discoveries in astronomy in the sixteenth century, the mechanical model of nature was the clock. In the period of the Industrial Revolution the model for nature was changed from that of a clock to an engine. Today it is the computer, not just the one I have sitting on my desk, but an infinitely more complex computer.

Biologists around the world are trying to create with their computers an 'artificial reality', an 'artificial life' and an 'artificial consciousness'. For example, the way, they say, to settle the question of how the mind works is to build a working mind. That is something you could then test and measure. You can get your teeth into it. The ecologist no longer needs to be a field person dealing with real live plants and animals. He can create a digital habitat on his computer and let loose digital organisms to procreate, mutate and evolve in it. He has invented artificial evolution as well as artificial ecology. In all these examples there is a simple reduction of minds to information. Is life then just information? The nerds of the movie *Jurassic Park* created dinosaurs who ran around on the screen. Is that life or is it engineering? Mechanism is not a solution to the problem of the universe but a strategy. Like all strategies it works within the sphere of battle it is designed for. But its proponents are not that precise in identifying the battlefield where they draw their stakes. As Mary Midgley (1992) has pointed out in another context: 'As usual in these scientific fantasies, Jekyll and Hyde seem to seize the word-processor by turns' (p. 196).

Some have called the use of computers as models of reality a third culture or nerd culture, the first two cultures being regular science and the arts. C. P. Snow, who invented the phrase 'two cultures', in the second edition of his book introduced the notion of a third culture. He envisaged literary intellectuals conversing directly with scientists. This never happened. John Brockman, a literary agent for many bright scientists, resurrected and amended Snow's third culture to describe something that was happening, namely working scientists communicating directly with lay people and the lay people challenging them back. And that is happening today. This particular sort of third culture is nerd culture.

There is a proposition for distinguishing between 'tough-minded' and 'tender-minded' people which I think was suggested by William James. A man is presented with what for all the world looks like a beautiful young woman. The man is then told that she is a robot, yet with all the features and qualities of a woman. There is no difference between her and a real woman. Would you make love to her? The tough-minded man says yes please. The tender-minded person says no thank you. Perhaps the distinction is not so black and white as this. There are probably degrees of tender and tough mindedness. The man who rejects William James' robot may well be aroused by a two-dimensional picture in an erotic magazine. You don't have to be robotic all the way. Some 'compuhype' takes the form of envisaging the eventual triumph of virtual sex over the real thing, including 'haptic' simulations (what bodies feel like to touch) (Kurzwell 1998).

The modern nerd has no doubt that eventually his robots will have feelings. If you could build a robot that was physically exactly like a person then the claim is that it would have feelings. The reason for his assurance is that the nerd starts with the assumption that the human body is completely mechanical and all you have to do is get the machinery right. If the robot hasn't got feelings there is something wrong with the machinery. That is the quintessence of reductionism or tough-mindedness applied to humans. Two questions need to be distinguished. Can machines duplicate the intelligent behaviour of humans? And can machines duplicate the inner subjective experience of humans? The answer to the first question is yes. Brains are already being outdone in speed of calculation, data storage, theorem proving and chess. However, the simulation of intelligent behaviour is not the simulation of inside feelings. Computation is not the simulation of mentality in both its aspects. Computation is but one aspect of mentality. Bear in mind also that the robot is made of silicon chips. The chips are made of atoms and molecules. But they are not the atoms and molecules as complexly organised in living cells. The robotic assumption is that the pseudo-cells made of chips are functionally the same as living cells. But of course they are not. At the most they are very approximate models with many missing elements. Kurzwell (1998) offers us a vision of the future when we shall be able to unload our mind into a suitable computing machine. This would be a way of improving our computing abilities and achieving a sort of immortality. In contemplating this possibility Colin McGinn (1999) comments: 'I for one would prefer sentient mortality to insentient immortality' (p. 12).

The tough-minded scientist is a mechanist through and through. He usually denies that he has any metaphysical beliefs at all. Yet mechanism is as much a metaphysical belief as is panexperientalism or any other organismic philosophy. Two prominent tough-minded biologists are Richard Dawkins and James Watson. The tender-minded biologist is more likely to admit that his metaphysical stance influences his science. One of them, C. H. Waddington, has written a paper on how his metaphysical convictions, derived from A. N. Whitehead, influenced both the sorts of problems he studied and the manner in which he tried to solve them (Waddington 1969). Other examples of tender-minded biologists are Brian Goodwin, Sewall Wright, Mae-Wan Ho and Rupert Sheldrake. I find in them a rich soup compared with the thin gruel of mechanism pure and simple. In defending his position that his metaphysics had influenced his research Waddington wrote:

> And that point I have I think established, even if you feel that my metaphysics has led me up the garden path. And, after all, I am a biologist; it is plants and animals that I am interested in, not clever

> exercises in algebra or even chemistry. The garden path has its
> attractions for the likes of us, and all of us who want to understand
> living systems in the more complex and richer forms are fated to
> look like suckers to our colleagues who are content to make a quick
> (scientific) buck wherever they can build up a dead-sure pay-off. (p. 81)

René Descartes was both an engineer and a biologist. He was the first great thinker who was struck by the peculiarity of inner experience. Hence his famous statement, 'I think therefore I am.' A more accurate English version is, 'I am consciously aware, therefore I know that I must exist.' Let Descartes speak for himself, as quoted by Whitehead (1929a p. 41): 'Let it be so; still it is at least quite certain that it seems to me that I see light, that I hear noise and that I feel heat. That cannot be false; properly speaking it is what is in me called feeling (*sentire*); and used in this precise sense that is no other thing than thinking.' Descartes was surely right about this, that there is nothing we are more certain of than our own conscious experience.

Descartes was not so right when he said the world was made of two different sorts of substances—matter and mind. The universe and all its parts were machines. Humans were machines with minds. Other living organisms and the atoms of which they were made were machines without minds. This is the famous Cartesian dualism—the bifurcation of nature into matter and mind, subject and object, observer and observed. It reinforced the reductionist analysis of science. As I have already indicated, much of the success of modern science was precisely due to its sharp delineation of its subject matter, excluding all subjective aspects. This sort of surgery worked well for a time. It meant that science tackled the problems that could be defined and for which answers could be found. In this sense the abstraction was a happy one. It has allowed the simplest things to be considered first. It is time now to move on.

The abstraction of modern science, or what can correctly be called the modern worldview, has led to a mistaken idea of how science does its work. We say the method of science is objective. It has nothing to do with values or emotions. It looks at the world as it really is. When you come to analyse what this means it becomes nonsense. It is not true that we observe best when we are entirely devoid of emotion. Unless there is a direct interest and a passionate one, we do not observe at all. Charles Darwin commenced his voyage around the world in the *Beagle* as a collector of natural history specimens for the British Museum. That would be a pretty limiting occupation if that were where it ended. But it didn't. He got interested in ideas about variation in animals and plants that led to tentative hypotheses as to the origin of adaptive variation. Very soon, he tells us, he never went into the field (be that a jungle or a seashore) without having some hypothesis in mind. These hypotheses became his passionate interest without which he would have missed observing many things.

Great scientists I have known or known about were passionate observers. There is nothing objective about that. Barbara McClintock won a Nobel Prize for her work on the genetics of corn plants. She tells us (McDaniel 1986): 'I start with the seedling, and I don't want to leave it. I don't feel I really know the story if I don't watch the plant all the way along. So I know every plant in the field. I know them intimately, and I find it a real pleasure to know them' (p. 34). Her feeling for the organism was that of a fellow subject. She seemed to have a passionate involvement. I can recall the leader of a research team financed from the Rockefeller Foundation to eliminate the yellow fever mosquito from South America saying that he had to put himself in the place of a mosquito and think like a mosquito. Where can I get my next blood meal? Where do I rest while maturing my eggs? Where do I lay my eggs? And so on. Having interviewed several reputed scientists of the late twentieth century on television about the sources of their creativity, Wolpert and Richards (1997) transcribed the interviews in an engaging book appropriately entitled *Passionate Minds*. The top scientists are passionate. Passion is a major component of their creativity. Despite the intrusion of emotion and passion into the method of science, its exponents nevertheless believe they are discovering objective nature because their model is that of a machine without subjective qualities. The outstanding example of this today in biology is molecular biology, as I indicate below.

Some of the great feuds in science were a result of passionately held beliefs. Pythagoras adhered passionately to a belief in the universality of rational numbers. It was said that he became so incensed when his disciple proved the square root of 2 at least to be an exception that he had the young man killed. More recently this century a public endorsement of Mendelian genetics was enough to earn Russian geneticists a one-way trip to the Gulag and Heisenberg's affirmation of quantum mechanics came close to doing something similar for him in 1937.

Molecular biology is the theophany of reductionism in which biological entities are reduced to molecules. Some molecular biologists believe that the total description of a human being will be in terms of the total description of the person's DNA. The DNA constitution of humans as a whole is called the human genome. One biology textbook says the human being is nothing but a complex biochemical mechanism powered by a combustion system which energises computers with prodigious storage facilities for retaining encoded information. The mistake is the exclusive phrase 'nothing but'. It is saying that the living organism is nothing but physics and chemistry. The ardent molecular biologist wants to take over the rest of biology. Most of it, they claim, is nothing more than stamp collecting. E. O. Wilson, who is both an ecologist and sociobiologist, tells of putting up a proposition to appoint an ecologist to the staff of the Biological Laboratories at Harvard University where he was professor. Molecular biologist and Nobel Prize laureate James Watson said to the meeting, 'Are they out of their minds?' 'What do you mean?' asked Wilson. 'Anyone who would hire an ecologist is out of his mind,' replied Watson (Wilson 1994 p. 220).

In the university as a whole reductionism has led to the creation of separate departments of knowledge and a consequent disciplinolatory. Yet the real student abhors boundaries. A task of the future is to create a university without boundaries. The Harvard philosopher W. V. Quine said that boundaries are for deans and libraries. If only that were the case!

The principle of reductionism is the analysis of things down to their component parts so as to build them again into the original entity, be it a solar system or a human being. In so doing you always get a machine. It is exactly what one might do in analysing a motor car into its component bits and pieces. You would get a pile of nuts, screws, rivets and complex shapes of metal. From the pile of bits you could, if you knew the blueprint of the motor car, build it up again from its parts. In the process of attempting to do that with the human, what happens to feelings and consciousness? They get left out. They disappear as did the cat in the Viennese joke at the beginning of this chapter. Hence Wordsworth's 'We murder to dissect'. Reductionism of the living is to cut people and other creatures down to size, to something that can be measured.

There is a fundamental difference between a machine and an organism. In a machine pre-existing parts are assembled together into a functional unity such as a clock or a motor car. An organism is different. The parts of an organism—leaves, roots, flowers, limbs, eyes, hearts and brains—are not made independently and then assembled as in a machine. They arise as a result of interactions between developing parts which are molecules, cells, tissues and organs. The organism is not just a structural unity. It is a functional unity as well. The parts exist by virtue of developing relationships with one another in relation to the whole functioning organism. Another approach is not to let the subjective disappear completely but to say that it is real but beyond comprehension. Philosophers with this latter view call themselves noumenists.

THE OBJECTIVE AND THE SUBJECTIVE

Science as we know it inevitably leads to mechanical analyses. Is there nothing more to be said? I think there is. It is to propose that there are two points of view—*the inside and the outside, the subjective and the objective, from within and from without.* One cannot be reduced to the other. There is the patient's point of view of her kidney colic and that of the doctor who investigates it. The patient can also be the doctor. Every medical complaint has objective or physical aspects. Equally there is always a psychological or subjective side, even if it be only how people cope with illness and pain. There is an enormous gap between what science describes and what we experience. There is need for greater understanding as to how to bring the inner and the outer together. Indeed the solution to the riddle of life is only possible through the proper connection of the outer with the inner experience.

No-one can truly feel another person's inner feelings, though we can empathise with them. The only individual any of us knows with much intimacy is oneself and a few other humans. This inevitable separation of ourselves from others has a good side and a bad side. The good side is that each of us has an inalienable right to privacy. The bad side is a loneliness which some can't cope with. I alone and afraid in a world I never made. One solution is to replace loneliness with the positive experience of solitude. Bertrand Russell lived a life which seemed to his biographer to be a perpetual oscillation between the pain of extreme aloneness on the one hand and the joy of solitude on the other. He came home one day after hearing a moving lecture by Professor Gilbert Murray on one of Plato's dialogues. There he found his dear friend Mrs Evelyn Whitehead suffering a very severe bout of pain. She seemed to Russell to be cut off from everyone and everything by walls of agony. The sense of aloneness of each human soul suddenly overwhelmed him. He wrote that the loneliness of the human soul is unendurable. 'Nothing can penetrate it,' he said, 'except the highest intensity of love that religious teachers have preached.' This experience of the aloneness of each soul led Russell to feel that in human relationships one should penetrate to the core of loneliness in each person and speak to that. For a time, he said, 'that sort of mystic illumination possessed me' (Monk 1997 p. 135). He began to feel in far closer touch with his friends than previously. He called this his moment of conversion. Bertrand Russell had a second string to his bow in dealing with his aloneness. That was his retreat into the 'profundities of mathematics' which became totally fulfilling at the time and which culminated in the monumental work with A. N. Whitehead, *Principia Mathematica*.

We are not the only creatures who have an inner and an outer, a subjective and an objective, side to our lives. As I try to understand the behaviour of a non-human animal such as my cat there is the objective or scientific information about stimulus and response but there is also the question: what is it like to be a cat? I can't have the cat's experience but I can surmise about it. Likewise with the birds who visit me every day on my balcony. I may ask why they sing. The objective answer is to establish a territory, to attract a mate or to warn off predators. All that is true. I can also ask another question: do they sing to enjoy themselves like us, and if not why not? That question is more difficult, yet not completely opaque to investigation.

As a student of biology I was brought up to avoid being anthropomorphic, that is, to think of other creatures in human-like terms. That was a mistake. I now ask-why should I not be anthropomorphic? We do not really know what it is qualitatively like to be a cat, let alone an atom, but only what it is like to be a human person. I have my own private experience which no-one else has. It is my inward private view of the world. There is then a perfectly logical reason for looking to human experience as such to furnish a model of reality rather than to the models of classical physics alone. We can share our objective knowledge about ourselves which is public knowledge. But we can go further. We can surmise about another person's subjective feelings. And if it is okay to surmise that other humans have feelings, why not for cats and birds? I know no reason why not (Birch 1995).

Quantum physics has departed from the Newtonian mechanistic paradigm, so much so that it knows no models other than those of quite abstract mathematics. Biology is still in the mechanistic age of Newtonian physics. I am not sure why—physics' envy of a physics of substances maybe. Just over one hundred years ago (in 1887) J. J. Thomson discovered the electron and said you could not really know what an electron was unless you were one. There is something *it is like to be*. Discoveries in physics led to the concept that we do not really know what the fundamental entities, such as electrons, are. The best we can do is to make models of them which are mathematical abstractions. Nevertheless, Thomson recognised that there is something beyond all models that needs to be taken into account. More recently physicists such as David Bohm speculate what the nature of this inner aspect may be.

In her book, *Limerence*, Dorothy Tennov tells us about the subjective side of being in love. To understand the objective side we can turn to books such as Anthony Walsh's *The Science of Love*. There we learn that the euphoria of falling in love is associated with dopamine, phenylethylamine (PEA) and other chemical substances. PEA is said to give love's special kick. Sooner or later the kick peters out. Another set of chemicals seems to be associated with enduring love that hopefully follows. These are the endomorphins. When a lover is abandoned the absence of endomorphins results in despondency and a broken heart which are withdrawal symptoms. It would be true to say that the experience of falling in love involves the release of various chemicals into the bloodstream. These are objective *correlates* of the subjective experience of falling in love. But falling in love is not to be described solely in terms of dopamine, phenylethylamine and other chemicals. They are not the whole phenomenon, which includes the particular feeling—falling in love.

A prevalent cause of human suffering is depression. One approach to the study of depression is to understand the neurobiology and endocrinology of this emotion along lines analogous to the analysis of the science of love. Our knowledge of the neural correlates of various forms of depression has vastly increased in recent years. For example, in at least some forms of depression there is a modulation of neurotransmitters such as serotonin, noradrenalin and dopamine whose levels can be manipulated by antidepressive drugs. But there is also the subjective approach to understanding depression which a psychiatrist may approach through means such as cognitive and group therapy. Or we may try to evoke in ourselves appropriate and positive thoughts such as realising that the present experience of anxiety is not the end of the world for us.

I remember my first professor of zoology telling the class that the healthy animal is up and doing. That applies to us too. Our most valuable motivation to be up and doing is interest. Interest leads to excitement. This goes two ways. It can lead to the objective phenomena of vandalism, rioting, bullying and graffiti-spraying. They are popular because they are interesting and perhaps even exciting when you have nothing better to do. Euphoric drugs come into this category. The second side of interest and excitement is that it can be directed to creative acts. A central task of any society is to direct interest away from the destructive towards the creative. Maybe there is a biology of interest and excitement waiting to be discovered. Perhaps these subjective qualities may one day be found to have their correlates in specific neurochemical transmitters. But these chemicals will be correlates, not the experience itself. It is too easy to forget that.

We think of ourselves as conscious, free, feelingful, rational agents in a world that mechanistic science tells us consists entirely of mindless, meaningless physical particles. That's the gap we need to try to fill if we are really to know what it is to be a human or to be a cat or an electron.

The model we have of what it is to be human has important practical implications in the real world in which we live our daily lives. Consider, for example, how a reductionist orientation may affect the practice of medicine. Victor Frankl, who was a psychiatrist, argued that exclusive belief in reductionism, be that belief conscious or unconscious, has an effect on mental health. He tells us that he had more and more patients who had a feeling of inner emptiness and sense of the meaningless of their lives—what he calls an existential vacuum. He sees this as a direct denial of the subjective. A human being is not one thing among other things just pushed around by external forces. The sort of person a prisoner in Auschwitz became, said Frankl (himself an inmate), was the consequence of an inner decision and not the result of camp influences alone. It is what we bring to the crisis and not the crisis itself which determines the outcome (Frankl 1969).

HOW TO BRING THE SUBJECTIVE AND THE OBJECTIVE TOGETHER

I have referred to the view from the outside and the view from the inside. Can we hold both together in a unified view? Consider stereoscopic vision. There is a difference between the right and the left pictures that are offered to us by our left and our right eye. It is the difference that mediates a new wholeness, an additional dimension. What holds for vision is true of life in general. We need the objective scientific analysis together fused with the inner subjective view. The apartheid solution is no solution.

How to integrate the two into a worldview? Materialism is dead. So too is vitalism. Vitalism supposed that living things had a vital spirit lacking in non-living things. So let's start again. We need another sort of conceptual tool kit. If mind and spirit grow out of matter it is our conception of matter that needs revision. A proposition of process thought is that in addition to interpreting the higher in terms of the lower (reductionism or the bottom up approach) is the interpretation of the lower in terms of the higher (the top down approach). First it means acknowledging that human experience is a real subjective fact. Secondly, it is to see human experience as a high-level example of reality in general. The proposition is that experience is a feature of the life of birds and lizards and amoebae and, yes, all the way down. The alternative is a world of vacuous actualities, bits and pieces like billiard balls. That is, a mechanistic universe as opposed to a feeling organic universe.

Life does not make a living organism the way a builder makes a cathedral with stones neatly piled one upon another. You can tear down the cathedral and from the pile of stones you can build a house or another cathedral. A living organism is not like that at all. A living organism can indeed be broken down into its component parts, but the whole has properties that the components do not have. The properties of the whole are not found in the parts except they be organised in that whole. It is for this reason that the reductionist program is deficient. One response has been to say that the whole is more than the sum of the parts. There is an element of truth in this statement. But it does not go far enough. It is not just that the whole is more than the sum of its parts. Rather it is that the parts become qualitatively different by being parts of a whole. That is basically the difference between a machine, such as a computer, and ourselves. The parts of a computer laid out separately on a bench are not changed when they are assembled into a computer. Computers have a merely aggregational, not a subjective or experiential unity. Griffin (1998) asks this question concerning the possibility of computers having consciousness and freedom:

> Could, for example, consciousness arise from complexly organised silicon chips? From a panexperientialist perspective, on the one hand, this possibility could not be ruled out on the grounds that silicon atoms, being devoid of experience, could not give rise to conscious experience. Such atoms, by hypothesis, do have a lowly type of experience ... On the other hand, a direct jump from silicon (or any other simple) atoms to human-like experience, with its consciousness and freedom, would be impossible. There is presumably a reason that it took some four billion years for that kind of transformation to occur in the evolutionary process. The reason suggested here is that the intervening levels of experience were necessary. Human-like consciousness could only develop out of a central nervous system composed of units with the experiential complexity of eukaryotic cells; eukaryotic cell-like experiences could only emerge out of things with as much experiential richness as organelles; and so on down. So, for a computer to enjoy consciousness and freedom, it would have to have something like a brain composed of units something like the cells of our brains ... What does seem necessary is that the brain be composed of billions of compound individuals with a complexity and corresponding experiential richness like unto that of our own brain cells. Because fabricated things with these characteristics would be so different from any computers actual or even remotely possible today

as to require another name, we can say that, from this perspective, computers cannot have freedom, consciousness, or any level of unified experience. (pp. 197–8)

This quotation contains an idea which is fundamental. Atoms and molecules don't just get assembled in the twinkling of an eye into something that thinks and feels in a rich experience. There are rites of passage, first through complex molecules, then organelles (which become parts of cells), then cells and so on. Each level has its own degree of freedom and subjectivity but not that yet of the human being. Yet traditional mechanistic biology promotes the idea that very late in the evolutionary process a rich level of experience emerges, maybe in birds, but more usually proposed in mammals.

It is easy to describe the properties of atoms in the language of physics, of molecules in the language of chemistry, of cells in the language of biology. But it is not so easy to provide the translation rules for moving from one language to another. This is because as one moves up a level the properties of each larger whole are given not merely by the units of which it is composed but by the organising relations between them. This means that the properties of matter relevant at one level are just inapplicable to other levels. My interpretation of this is that the individual entities, be they electrons or molecules, for example, are themselves different by virtue of being parts of a whole. A cell in the brain is not the same as a brain cell in tissue culture. It is objectively different. For one thing it has a different shape. I presume it also is subjectively different because of its different internal relationships.

The technical term for this relationship between the part and the whole is that the *internal relations* of an entity, be that entity a human being or an electron, determine the nature of that entity. It is what it is by virtue of its internal relations to its environment. which obviously means other entities. Whitehead (1929a) put it this way, that the philosophy of organism is mainly devoted to the task of making clear the notion of 'being present' in another entity (p. 50). He borrowed this phrase from Aristotle but gave it a different meaning. He goes on to say that the phrase for Aristotle suggested the crude notion that one entity is added to another. That is not what Whitehead meant. What he meant is that one entity is constituted by its relationship to other entities, which is very different. This is a very important distinction because some critics of Whitehead make a caricature by claiming that all he is doing is pasting mind onto atoms. Nothing of the sort.

You don't really know what the physicist's fundamental units are until you see them organised into a complex organism such as a human. It is for this reason that one day biology will take over physics and not physics take over biology. Life is more than physics and chemistry. Perhaps it may take another thousand years. But we can be part of a vanguard moving in that direction, even if at times it seems to be moving at a glacial pace.

THE 'CASH VALUE' OF AN ORGANIC-RELATIONAL VIEW OF NATURE

William James was keen on asking what was the 'cash value' of ideas. He didn't mean some sort of cost–benefit analysis. What he meant was after all the weighing, debating and promotion of any particular idea or approach is done, what difference does it make? We are right to ask this question of the rather radical ideas presented in this chapter. What cash value have they in a postmodern world? There are a number.

First, a feature of life in the modern world for many people is a sense of profound emptiness. There are doubtless many reasons for this. It was at one time taken for granted that the fruits of science, industrialisation and mechanisation would bring happiness and fulfilment to all humankind. Those who so reasoned did not understand the limits of science and technology. It was hoped that science would free us from superstition. It was hoped that technology would free us from poverty and the struggle for the means of existence. Science did indeed free us from many superstitions such as witchcraft and the like. But into that vacuum came other superstitions or misbeliefs such as extreme materialism on the one hand and on the other hand fundamentalist religion. Technology did indeed free us from much poverty. It showed us how to get rich. For many, the accumulation of riches became a religion in itself. What has now become important is the need for convictions about the meaning of human life, what it is to be human and how our lives can be fulfilled. That means that at the very basis of life we need to look beyond the dominant worldview of materialism to a worldview that stresses values such as purpose, freedom and creativity. Science in its modern phase since the Industrial Revolution had been so successful in tackling the problems it has set itself that we tend to accept the materialistic philosophy that has been built upon it. We can only gain by looking beyond that limited boundary.

Second, the transformation of a scientific worldview that is non-materialistic has begun in the new physics. It has transformed physics into a wholistic and exciting view of reality. Its extension to biology is a necessary requirement if our total world view is to be more organic and less mechanic. And from biology we extend it to social studies. Biology is waiting for such an understanding. Some of the components of such a view have been discussed in this chapter. As for social studies the materialism that is with us now has been an alibi for all sorts of materialistic ideologies in capitalism, socialism, economics and other social theories. They have their goals in the acquisition of power and wealth. What then is powerful enough to provide ideas for a new goal of the common good of humankind? One human activity that is successful in unifying effort to a chosen end is war. Whole societies are then galvanised into a unitary effort. How then can societies be galvanised into effort for the common good of humankind and the world? William James coined the phrase 'the moral equivalent of war' to describe that high level of motivation that would be transforming. In history radical changes have centred around charismatic and insightful people with ideas such as Mahatma Gandhi of India and Nelson Mandela of South Africa. Gandhi recognised what he called seven social sins and worked to rectify each one. They are: politics without principles, wealth without work, pleasure without conscience, knowledge without character, commerce without morality, science without humanity, and worship without sacrifice.

Gandhi and Mandela had ideas for a new world which they pursued with riveted zeal and great sacrifice. Things can change. But we have to have ideas that fill us with enthusiasm. We need purpose and passion together with the know-how. Nor do we have to wait for the whole world to be changed. I recall Margaret Mead saying: 'Never doubt what a small group of thoughtful committed citizens can do to change the world. Indeed, it is the only thing that ever has.'

Third, we need a philosophy which is coherent with the promotion of the multicultural society. Some forms of genetic determinism run counter to this objective. A non-racist society need be based on a non-racist interpretation of biology. This is pursued in chapter 4.

Fourth, we need a philosophy which is coherent with environmentalism. It will insist on a relational approach. An important component of such a philosophy is the attribution of intrinsic value to creatures besides ourselves who share the Earth with us. An organic view of nature provides such an understanding (chapter 5).

Fifth, we need a philosophy which is coherent with a non-sexist society. It will reach out to feminism and the male counterpart to help in building a society free of gender inequities. A proper understanding of biology supports such a goal.

Sixth, we need a religion which is naturalistic as distinct from supernaturalism. This subject is developed in chapter 6.

The above is not a list of solutions but rather an agenda for a future based on a relational and process view of the world and all that is in it.

4

CUTTING HUMANS
DOWN TO SIZE

> Build thee more stately mansions, O my soul,
>   As the swift seasons roll!
>   Leave thy low-vaulted past!
> Let each new temple, nobler than the last,
> Shut thee from heaven with a dome more vast,
>   Till thou at length art free,
> Leaving thine outgrown shell by life's unresting sea!
>
> Oliver Wendell Holmes, 'The Chambered Nautilus'

Procrustes in Greek legend was a robber of Attica who placed all who fell into his hands upon an iron bed. If they were longer than the bed he cut off the overhanging parts, if shorter he stretched them till they fitted.

Some exponents of science, particularly in popular literature, are Procrustians. Their reductionism cuts people down to size. Genetic determinism is the most common way of doing this in our time. This is the thesis that how we are brought up and the nature of our family background have little effect on the sort of people we become. The main aspects of our personality and behaviour are preordained by our genes. So intervention by social workers into our lives would not solve our problems. Instead, we should promote interventions in human biology to mitigate our problems. We can blame the poor, the hungry and oppressed for their unhappy condition rather than the failure of the economic system or the government to secure a decent life for all. This is an old doctrine of human nature in a new dress of genetics. Genetic determinism has been an alibi for socialism, for capitalism and for racism. It is now an alibi for all sorts of human behaviour. A man is homosexual because he is supposed to have a 'gay gene' that causes him to have a 'gay brain'. Genes, it is claimed, are responsible for alcoholism, criminality, violence, schizophrenia, intelligence and a host of other behavioural traits. Even a mood gene has been suggested. In the last analysis what determines us is our biology. This is the message of what has become called sociobiology or latterly 'evolutionary psychology' (e.g., Ridley 1998). These doctrines give great sovereignty to genes in determining our behaviour. It is easy to see how this emphasis relocates social problems in the individual rather than exploring their social roots. In their bestseller, *The Bell Curve,* Charles Murray and Richard Herrnstein suggested that a biologically deprived underclass had emerged in our society. DNA is becoming the last court of appeal. In a 1994 trial of a young American accused of murder the defence argued for leniency on the grounds: 'You don't fault a blind person because he can't read the road signs, you don't fault a deaf person because he can't hear what you are saying ... And if there is a biochemical basis ... it's not justifying it, but it is mitigating' (Jones 1997b p. xiii). The murderer can say, it was not me it was my genes. But is this good science? The direct answer is no. There is no hard scientific credible evidence to give support to the doctrine of the dominance of genes in our behaviour. Steve Jones (1997b p. xiii) remarks that no-one disputes that social position is inherited. The chances of being in *Who's Who* is one in five for those whose father is included, but one in fifteen hundred for the general population. Enthusiasts for genetic determinism might claim that this is written into our DNA, but is it? Human nature and our human characteristics are an expression simultaneously of biological and social components. To understand that we need to know the relation between gene, organism and environment.

GENE, ORGANISM AND ENVIRONMENT

Humans and chimpanzees have much of their genes in common. The main differences between them and us are due to the genes that differ. Some of the differences between people are due to differences in their genes. I have blue eyes because I inherited genes for blue eyes from my mother. There are many so-called genetic diseases that seem to have a unitary genetic cause. Cystic fibrosis and Huntington's chorea are rare diseases that occur in people carrying the relevant mutant gene. Their expression is independent of occupation, social class or education. It is this sort of information that led a world leader in molecular biology to claim in his opening address to a scientific congress that if he had a large enough computer and the complete

DNA sequence of an organism he could compute the organism, by which he presumably meant he could describe its anatomy, physiology and behaviour. This has been exhaustively argued by Richard Lewontin who concludes 'But that is wrong' (Lewontin 1993 p. 63).

Besides the rather clear-cut examples of genetic disease such as cystic fibrosis, the expression of other genetic diseases is more sensitive to environment. For example, sickle-cell anaemia in West Africans has severe effects only under physical stress. In general at any moment of its life a living organism is a consequence of a developmental history that results from the interaction of internal and external forces. The internal forces include the genes. They do not act autonomously but in response to external forces. These are its environment. For example, the enzyme that breaks down lactose sugar to provide energy for bacterial growth is only manufactured by bacterial cells when they detect the presence of lactose in their environment. Thus genes are turned on or off depending upon their environment. There is a second internal component which Lewontin (1992) refers to as developmental noise. Developmental noise accounts for the fact that identical twins, called identical because they have identical genes, have different fingerprints and that our fingerprints are different on our left and right hand. Every cell in the hand has identical genes and has had the same environment during development. This variation between fingerprints is thought to be due to random movements of the cells and chance molecular events within the cells during the development of the organism. This aspect of development alone is reason for rejecting absolute genetic determinism.

Even if we knew the complete molecular specification of every gene in an organism we could not predict what that organism would be. We might be able to tell the difference between a chimpanzee and a human because these differences are almost entirely due to the difference in genes. But variation between individuals within a species such as ourselves is a consequence of genes, environment and developmental noise. All are important. Because three components are involved in the making of ourselves, some have thought it might be possible to partition what we owe to the different components. For example, it has commonly been proposed that in a population of people, 80 per cent of the differences in intelligence between them is caused by their genes and 20 per cent by their environment (figures notoriously based on what is now known to be faked research data of Sir Cyril Burt). Although this statement sounds plausible enough it is fallacious. The proportion of variation in a population as a consequence of variation in genes is not a fixed property but one that varies from environment to environment. There are many diseases in which a defective gene results in defective physiology. There is a maleficent gene which, if inherited from both parents, deprives its possessor of the power to metabolise the ubiquitous protein constituent phenylalanine. This leads to gross defects in the development of the nervous system and to low grade mental deficiency. About 1 per cent of mentally defective individuals are victims of this inborn error of metabolism known as phenylketonuria. If, however, the disease is diagnosed shortly after birth and the child is fed a diet nearly free of phenylalanine then the offending gene has no opportunity to make itself manifest. The environment determines the expression of the gene. Another example is Wilson's disease, which is a genetic defect that prevents its sufferers from detoxifying copper they consume in minute quantities in normal food. The copper builds up in the body and eventually causes degeneration of the nerves and finally death. This can indeed be described as a genetic disorder. However, people with this defective gene can lead perfectly normal lives and have a normal development by taking a pill that helps them to get rid of the copper and they are indistinguishable from anyone else. The gene is what it is and does what it does by virtue of its environment. In the much publicised genes 'for' breast cancer and heart disease there are plenty of people with the genes but not the disorder and plenty of others with the disorder but not the gene.

A change in the cultural environment of people can greatly affect their apparent intelligence. Any ordinary primary school student in the Western world can add a column of figures correctly and more quickly than the most intelligent mathematician in Ancient Rome who had to struggle with cumbersome X's, V's and I's. A change in the cultural environment in this case changes abilities by many orders of magnitude. This is no basis for supposing that an Australian child with a pocket computer today is more intelligent than a mathematician in Ancient Rome. Differences that are ascribed to genes in one environment may disappear completely in another.

Newspapers report on the discovery of a gene for this or that 'trait'. How terrible we say to have a gene for this or that disorder if it is a disorder. This is muddled genetalk that takes no account of the interaction between gene, organism and environment. At one stage it was popular to report a gene for homosexuality. One investigator said he had found it on the X chromosome (which comes from the mother) leading to the production of a T-shirt for gays which gave the details plus the expletive, 'Thanks Mom!' Well don't worry. Better to read chapter 11, 'Fascinating Genetalk', in Philip Kitcher's (1996) *The Lives to Come*. He warns us on how not to be misled by such media pronouncements.

Christina Rathbone (1997) spent a year as a visitor at a high school in west-side Manhattan and wrote of her experience in a book she called *On the Outside Looking In*. This was a school marooned by budget cuts. It existed on three floors of a mid-town highrise. It took in marginal teenagers mostly already rejected by other high schools. Rathbone sat in on classes and visited students in their homes, or on visits to jail and to gang meetings in Washington Heights. Students were involved in crack houses, dealing in heroin and beating up classmates. She became convinced as she got to know them that they would have had very different fates had they not been born into such grim circumstances. She saw good lives being wasted, not only by poverty but by society's inadequate response to it. The school was without a gym or cafeteria and with so few textbooks that students could not take them home. But she had some successes—a boy reading his first book, a girl leaving a gang to take her first job, another girl getting top grades even as she dealt with the pain of years of sexual abuse. This is a story of how economic injustice leads to social deprivation and stunted lives and how in some cases a bit of extra care and concern can help to reverse the direction of lives. Rathbone concluded that what separates the poor from the rest of society is the difference in where they were born, and to whom. That is the emphasis that matters, not what genes they have or have not.

A similar conclusion has been reached by health workers in the UK. According to Helen Epstein (1998) if England were divided into two nations, one containing the richer regions and the other the poorer regions, there would be 80,000 more deaths every year in the poorer nation. Compared to the rich, the poor in Britain are more prone to about eighty different causes of death, including strokes, diabetes, accidents and mental illnesses such as depression and senile dementia. If you live in an industrial slum in Britain you are more likely to end up going to a bad school which prepares you mainly for unskilled jobs or unemployment. When you are sick you are more likely to see a doctor who would probably much rather be working elsewhere. Your most affordable forms of recreation would be smoking and television. Food is often more expensive in poor neighbourhoods. The nearby shops will probably be selling only canned and frozen foods. Britain introduced its National Health Service in 1948. While there was thereafter an overall improvement in health it failed to eliminate health inequalities. In 1991 death rates in the poorest 10 per cent of electoral wards in Britain were four time higher than they were in the richest 10 per cent. Something similar has been happening in the United States. Today life expectancy for males in generally poor urban areas such as the Bronx or Washington is ten to fifteen years lower than in richer districts such as Fairfax in Virginia or Douglas in Colorado. The underlying causes of these differences are much debated but Epstein assembles much evidence indicating that differences in the social environment are the critical elements. People who, for whatever reason, happen to be born into poor areas are destined to be less healthy. Their environment needs to be changed. Some aspects of this problem are also discussed in chapter 2 on quality of life in the workplace.

THE HUMAN GENOME PROJECT

The ultimate consequences of a belief in genetic determinism can be devastating. People are given visions of genes for alcoholism, violence and drug addiction that might ultimately be eliminated by gene substitution, whereas for these and other issues there is plenty of evidence that such maladies can be changed by a changed environment of the individual, which means change in society and its values. Belief in genetic determinism has led to the hugely expensive human genome project. It is the outcome of a belief that what we need to know about human beings is contained in their genes. The ultimate objective is to be able to write down the complete sequence of DNA in a human person. This final catalogue, costing billions of dollars to produce, will be a mosaic of some hypothetical average person corresponding to no-one in particular.

It is hoped that the information from the genome project will lead to gene therapy in people who appear to have defective genes. But the hopes of some go further when they suggest that we might not only be able to get rid of our bad genes but could with a bit of genetic engineering transplant good genes into people who want them. The term negative eugenics has been used for the process of eliminating bad genes. Positive eugenics is the promotion of what are regarded as good genes. Present effort is concentrated on negative genetics. And here there are two possible avenues of work. One is the elimination of deleterious genes in individuals suffering from some genetic disease. The other avenue, which is much more controversial, is genetic changes to the 'germ line'. The idea here, for example, is that if there is family history of a genetic disease then eliminate the bad genes in the sex cells so that the disease is not transmitted to subsequent generations. This approach is controversial because we do not know enough about how such a gene change might affect the development of the whole organism and our future evolution.

When Aldous Huxley wrote *Brave New World* in 1932 no-one imagined that science and technology know-how might one day make his vision reality. There are many problems. If diabetes, sickle-cell anaemia and cancer are to be prevented by altering genes, why not less serious disorders such as colour blindness, dyslexia and short stature? This raises the question as to what is defective. And behind this concept of defective lurks the image of a more perfect human. Who will decide what is good and what is defective or bad? Might parents wish to have genetic engineering enhance the intelligence or beauty of their offspring? Some genetic engineers consider that a future genetocracy is all but inevitable. Molecular biologist Lee Silver is reported to have spoken about two biological classes, Gen Rich and Naturals (Rifkin 1998). The Gen Rich include businessmen, musicians, athletes, intellectuals and others who are presumed to be society's elite. They have been enhanced with genes that enable to them to succeed in their chosen fields. Is engineered perfection a desirable thing? The answer very much depends upon our view of what it is to be human and to have a fulfilled life.

CLONING

William Blake's question, 'Little lamb who made thee?' might well be asked of lamb number 6LL3, better known as Dolly, of the Roslin Institute near Edinburgh. Three sheep went into the making of Dolly. There was the mother who supplied the egg that received an inserted nucleus from the udder of a second sheep. A third sheep provided the uterine environment in which the egg was transplanted. So Dolly had three mothers—nuclear mother, egg mother and womb mother. Dolly's DNA came from the implanted nucleus and also from the non-nuclear material of the ovum into which this nucleus was implanted. This is the DNA contained in the organelles known as mitochondria in the non-nuclear part of the cell. The role of this small amount of DNA is still uncertain. Dr Ian Wilmut, who did the research leading to Dolly, started with 277 eggs of which only one— Dolly—was truly successful. Others fell by the wayside. Further details and the ethical issues involved can be found in Pence (1998), *Flesh of my Flesh: The Ethics of Cloning Humans.*

Recognising that what is possible for sheep today will be feasible for humans tomorrow, commentators speculated on the legitimacy of cloning a Pavarotti or an Einstein or the chance of a demented dictator cloning an army of dictators. Polls showed that Mother Teresa was the most popular choice for person-to-be-cloned. But the film star Michelle Pfeiffer was not far behind. Perhaps we can blame Mary Wollstonecraft Shelley for much of the brouhaha over cloning. The Frankenstein story suggested that people can be made to order and that it will turn out to be disastrous. In the film version there is a riveting scene when the monster is brought to life. Dr Frankenstein roars, 'It's alive. Its alive. In the name of God ...' At that moment his lips keep moving but the voice disappears. The censors deleted the rest of the sentence—the forbidden words that have frightened cultures since ancient times: 'now I know what it feels like to be God'. But scientists don't want to be God. They want to solve scientific problems (Shermer 1999). Birth control? Only God can do that. Euthanasia? Only God can do that. Cloning? Only God can do that. In fact nature is already cloning humans. They are called identical twins. They have identical genes. But that doesn't make them identical. Identical genes do not make identical people, as was discussed earlier in this chapter. The genetically identical Dionne quintruplets did not turn out to be identical persons. Each had a different personality and life history (Lewontin 1998b). The notion of cloning an Einstein is a biological absurdity.

The desire of anyone to want to be cloned must surely be hubris to the nth degree. A motive for positive eugenics is to 'improve' on the present state of affairs. Cloning is the perpetuation of a present state of affairs. But not quite. Identical twins are not identical in all respects. Genetic identity does not determine personal identity. To think otherwise is to commit the fallacy of genetic determinism. Be that as it may, cloning in humans raises the problem of what right we have to decide what genes are bequeathed to 'offspring'. In normal reproduction what genes the offspring has is indeterminate and in large part a lottery. Cloning is different, for the genes of the cloned individual are the same as those of the individual who is cloned. The National Bioethics Advisory Commission of the USA recommended to the president against human cloning for the time being because they considered it was an unsafe procedure in humans. It also raised ethical issues; that cloning was a form of hubris, that it could lead to exploitation and oppression, that it would result in children being treated as objects, that it would damage the integrity of families and would threaten individuality and autonomy. These are all important issues. The British government advisory commission recommended that it would not be right at this stage to rule out limited research using cloning techniques which could be of great benefit to seriously ill people. The Australian Academy of Science (1999) made a similar recommendation. The proposed research would involve using a 'stem cell' from an early embryo and transplanting into it a nucleus from the sick person. It is conceivable that by identifying, say, the genes responsible for kidney production one might activate them to grow a kidney or some other organ. Another example would be to make nerve cells. The UK report and the Australian report were against cloning of a human being for safety and ethical reasons.

Similar recommendations were made by the World Health Organisation and the Council of Europe.

Like many social issues in biology, attitudes will change with time and more information. Immediate responses to technological break-throughs in biology are usually stereotyped. The furore that greeted the birth of Louise Brown, the world's first test-tube baby, now seems astonishing, generating fears that have now proved groundless. Perhaps in a decade the doom-saying response to Dolly the cloned sheep will appear equally overblown. On the other hand, the bland dismissal by many scientists of all social concerns as mere anti-science or 'genetic pornography' is equally blinkered. Those who are con-cerned often come to quite different conclusions as the next topic, sociobiology, shows.

SOCIOBIOLOGY

In 1975 Professor E. O. Wilson of Harvard University published *Sociobiology: The New Synthesis*, which immediately created a storm of both praise and criticism. Most of this book is a lucid account of social behaviour among many groups of animals. After twenty-six chapters of carefully documented biology of non-human animals comprising 94 per cent of the text there is final chapter entitled 'Man: From Sociobiology to Sociology'. The theme of this final chapter is that patterns of human social behaviour are under genetic control. Wilson speculates about the existence of genes for various behavioural traits in humans, that vary from person to person, such as aggression, xenophobia, homosexuality, religiosity and the differ-ences between men and women as well as many others. Three billion years of evolution of life have made us what we are. So we had bet-ter accept what evolution has made us unless we trust the human genome project to deliver us from our inborn ills. Wilson (1994) himself says:

> My argument ran essentially as follows. Human beings inherit a propensity to acquire behavior and social structures, a propensity that is shared by enough people to be called human nature. The defining traits include division of labor between the sexes, bonding between parents and children, heightened altruism toward closest kin, incest avoidance, other forms of ethical behavior, suspicion of strangers, tribalism, dominance orders within groups, male dominance over all, and territorial aggression over limiting resources. Although people have free will and the choice to turn in many directions, the channels of their psychological developments are nevertheless—however much we might wish otherwise—cut more deeply by the genes in certain

directions than in others. So while cultures vary greatly, they inevitably converge toward these traits. (pp. 332–3)

Wilson went on to say that the New Yorker and New Guinean highlander have been separated by 50,000 years of history but still understand each other, for the reason that their common humanity is preserved in the genes they share from their common ancestry. This seems to suggest that cultural history rather than genetics accounts for their differences, although the quote above says that genes cut more deeply in the differences. And elsewhere Wilson works hard to find genetic differences between different cultures (for a criticism see Gould 1987 p. 115).

The origin of altruistic behaviour is a problem for evolutionary biologists. Survival of the fittest suggests that evolution should maximise those qualities that lead to survival. The unfit go to the wall. Yet it is obvious that some individuals are altruistic and some are willing to lay down their lives for others. Could natural selection and survival of the fittest have made us genuinely cooperative and unselfish in pursuit of the greater good of others? I recall a lecture in the University of Chicago in the 1940s by the distinguished evolutionist Professor Sewall Wright on what he called the altruistic gene. This was a hypothetical gene that would cause its possessors to be altruistic. Wright put forward a genetic model of how such a gene might evolve and survive. Since then there have been many attempts to model the altruistic gene. An up-to-date account of where those attempts have got us is given by Richard Lewontin (1998) in his long essay review of a book on the subject by Sober and Wilson (1998) entitled *Unto Others: The Evolution and Psychology of Unselfish Behavior*. The orthodox view has been that altruistic behaviour could evolve when the altruistic individual contributes to the wellbeing of kin, the closer the kin the better. Natural selection in this case is acting not on the individual but on the group.

This idea has now been extended to groups beyond kin groups. Lewontin gives a striking example of selection between groups rather than between individuals in the story of the European rabbit in Australia. Rabbits were introduced into Australia in the nineteenth century for hunting. They quickly spread over huge areas of the continent with the exception of the tropics and became a serious pest. An attempt to control the rabbit was made by introducing from South America a viral disease, myxomatosis. In due course this spread rapidly and decimated much of the rabbit population. But the rabbits began to increase again. They had become genetically resistant to the disease organism. In addition, the disease organism had also evolved to be less virulent so that even susceptible rabbits survived the newly evolved virus. One might have thought that the more virulent strains of the virus would grow more quickly than the less virulent strains. But the trouble with being virulent is that the virus kills the rabbit. Myxomatosis is spread from rabbit to rabbit by mosquitoes and mosquitoes do not bite dead rabbits. So the virulent viruses guaranteed their own eventual elimination. Lewontin summarises the situation thus: 'Ethnic cleansing has been the pathway to national suicide and the more benign eventually survive globally'.

The outcome of a long argument on these lines is that any sort of group will do for this sort of evolution. All the viruses within a single rabbit are a group. So too is a group of animals that prefer one sort of food. Kin is a group. So the orthodox concept of kin selection leading to the evolution of altruism is swallowed up as a special case of selection between groups. Any group will do. So we are led to believe that the evolutionary process could lead to the accumulation of genes that tend towards altruistic behaviour. But this leaves open the question: what motivates the altruistic person to behave altruistically? Lewontin raises this question and asks the further question: is human altruism really egoism or even pure hedonism? The egoist asks: is it good for me? There may be some benefit to me by casting some bread upon the waters. The hedonist asks: does it feel good? Mark Twain wrote a book, *What Is Man?* in which he argued that all our actions are motivated by what makes us feel good. But the ethical question remains: what particular values make me feel good? One person may feel good hurting others. The ethical person feels good by helping others. The difference between these two sorts of ways of feeling good is fundamental. Which we display may be a consequence of our upbringing or even a sudden conversion from a negative way to positive one. We are not just products of our genes.

Clearly biology must have something to say about what we are. Humans are animals and have evolved by the same process as other animals. The debate is between those who argue that evolutionary biology can have little to say about human social behaviour and those who think that human social behaviour is to be understood primarily in terms of biology. As pointed out by Levine and Suzuki (1998 p. 222), part of the controversy springs from the nature of the research itself. In studying the genetics of human behaviour we are dealing with two most complex living systems: the human genome consists of at least 100,000 genes and the human brain contains more than 100 billion nerve cells. Understanding either is an enormous challenge. Predicting their interactions is extraordinarily difficult. It is therefore not surprising that causal links between genes and ill-defined traits such as 'intelligence' and 'aggression' and 'altruism' are exceedingly difficult to find. I have argued in this chapter that in considering any aspect of human behaviour such as aggression we approach the problem differently and propose that we have propensities for both aggression and for non-aggressive attitudes and how we can promote one over the other. The lion hardly has this choice. We have because we have more degrees of freedom to choose. It is all about whether there is such a thing as human nature, and if so what it is.

HUMAN NATURE

The issue of human nature is both vexed and complex. It is an issue at the back of all political ideas as to how society ought to be. How can we say anything about that unless we claim to know what human beings are really like? Apologists for unrestrained capitalism claim aggressiveness, entrepreneurial activity, male domination, territoriality and even xenophobia are innate in our nature and that determines what sort of society will work. Others more to the political left claim that we are really cooperative and altruistic underneath. Prince Kropotkin was a Russian anarchist who favoured a society based on voluntary cooperation between individuals, rejecting all forms of authority and coercion. He wrote the book *Mutual Aid* in which he argued for our innate cooperativeness. I recall visiting Jane Addams' famous Settlement House in Chicago. Hung on the wall behind her desk was (and probably still is) a portrait of Kropotkin. His views of human nature were an inspiration for her work amongst the deprived people, many of whom worked in the Chicago stockyards close by.

A radical alternative to each of these two positions is to deny the existence of human nature altogether. Human beings are simply what they make of themselves. In the hands of existentialists their denial of human nature leaves us with no way of understanding human society. It simply is what it is. There is yet a fourth position which makes more sense than any of the others. It is the proposition that we have propensities for almost any qualities in our lives. What we are depends upon the relation between organism gene and environment. That we now proceed to discuss.

We are inextricably part of nature. We share the same genetic code—the four-letter alphabet of A, G, C and T—with chimpanzees and bacteria and all the organisms in between. These letters spell out words which are the genes. Most of our genes we share with chimpanzees. But it does not follow that we are nothing but chimpanzee-like. The difference between us and chimpanzees is mainly in our genes, but the difference between modern humans and 'cavemen' of

100,000 years or so ago is in our culture. Biological evolution continues in our species but its rate is so slow compared with cultural evolution that its impact on human history has been small. In humans genetical evolution has been superseded by cultural evolution. The word 'culture' means information gained by one generation which is passed on to the next. In a sense invention makes the difference between the first humans and us; tools, machines, telephones, radio, television, supermarkets, schools and universities. Cultural evolution means that we are in control of that aspect of our evolution. Where genetic determinism fails is in attributing the difference between individuals and groups to genes, when it is largely cultural.

A claim of genetic determinists is that their critics are extreme cultural determinists. By this they mean that individuals are simply mirrors of the cultural forces that have acted on them from birth. Cultural determinists are said to believe that the organism at birth is a *tabula rasa*, a blank sheet on which culture and society can write anything. A corollary of cultural determinism is that we ought to be able to predict the character and actions of people from their social histories. But such is not the case. Our individual lives are the outcomes of a great multiplicity of intersecting causal pathways that involve both our genes and our environment. In some cases the emphasis may be on genes. In others it is on our cultural environment. There is no dichotomy between them.

A person with black skin is genetically different from a person with white skin. However, the differences that matter are not genetic but cultural. Some people are more aggressive in their behaviour than others. Aggression leads to wars. The genetic determinist says we do what we do because we are made that way. Some people are very peaceable and non-aggressive. Have their genes made them that way? To answer yes is to hark back to the old doctrine of original sin, but in modern dress. It says all have inherited the sin of Adam. If we are programmed to be what we are then these traits are ineradicable.

A reasonable hypothesis of this chapter that is more in keeping with the evidence than absolute determinism is that we have a potentiality both for aggressiveness and for non-aggressiveness. What we become depends upon our environment, which means our family, schooling and the society we live in. We can be changed. As Stephen J. Gould (1977) says: 'Our genetic makeup permits a wide range of behaviors—from Ebenezer Scrooge before to Ebenezer Scrooge after' (p. 266). It is a mistake to say we are innately miserly or aggressive when what we are depends so much on our environment. Gould (1981) has asked the following important question: 'What should be more adaptive for a learning and thinking animal: genes selected for aggression, spite and xenophobia; or selection for learning rules that can generate aggression in appropriate circumstances and peacefulness in others?' (p. 331). The latter proposition is sound both biologically and socially.

The old credo, 'You can't change human nature' is the modern credo of genetic determinists. Of course you can't change human nature if our nature is completely determined by our genes But to the extent that we are free to choose and therefore to make ethical decisions, biology is irrelevant. Biological determinism becomes a social weapon as Lewontin, Rose and Kamin (1984) pointedly argue:

> It is precisely because biological determinism is exculpatory that it has such wide appeal. If men dominate women, it is because they must. If employers exploit their workers, it is because evolution has built into us the genes for entrepreneurial activity. If we kill each other in war, it is the force of our genes for territoriality, xenophobia, tribalism, aggression. Such a theory can become a powerful weapon in the hands of ideologies who protect an embattled social organisation by 'a genetic defence of the free market'. It also serves at the personal level to explain individual acts of oppression and to protect the oppressors against the demands of the oppressed. It is 'why we do what we do' and 'why we sometimes behave like cavemen'. (p. 237)

In contrast to biological determinism the stance of the non-determinist is that there is a human nature which is simultaneously biologically and socially constructed.

The ethics of biological determinism is the ethics of the jungle. For example, in his book *On Human Nature*, E. O. Wilson (1978) considers that ways of life are worthy to the extent to which they serve the biological end of survival of the species. In Wilson's analysis, besides struggle for existence and survival of the fittest this could include certain sorts of altruistic behaviour which contribute to the greater survival of a group. However, such an ethic has nothing to say about any supreme moral action that does not contribute to the survival of the species. Wilson seems to have painted himself into the corner that Thomas Henry Huxley, Darwin's great protagonist, feared for himself. He asked whether human beings should embrace the way of life that got us here from our evolutionary forebears, namely the Darwinian principle of struggle for existence and survival of the fittest. He rejected that as a guide to human life, as we see below.

Since evolutionary success goes to those groups or species which contribute the greatest number of surviving offspring to each generation, sociobiologists ask how can human beings maximise the number of their descendants in future generations? The number of children a male can have is virtually limitless. However the number of children a female can have is strictly limited by the duration of pregnancy and the number of child-bearing years. The chances of survival of the offspring will depend amongst other things upon mating with a male who assists in providing for the offspring. Hence it is argued that a female can be expected to prefer a lasting relationship rather than a casual encounter. A male on the other hand may leave more descendants by mating with many females rather than just one. This, claims the sociobiologist, provides a biological basis for the double standard of sexual morality in conventional society. But as Peter Singer (1993) has pointed out, even if true this argument does not do anything to justify the existence of the double standard. It does nothing to justify the double standard as a moral truth. Singer makes the point that if males and females have a biological determinism in that direction it makes even stronger the case for making a deliberate decision now that we have understood it. Similarly sociobiological arguments for aggression do not justify aggression.

It is not enough to say my behaviour is in my genes, that Genes-R-Us. We can outfox what evolution has led us to. The point was made long ago by T. H. Huxley in his Romanes Lecture entitled 'Evolution and Ethics' delivered in the Sheldonian Lecture Theatre in Oxford in 1893. He argued that human cultural progress reverses the biological Darwinism of survival of the fittest. Social evolution is not to be achieved by a struggle for existence in which the weak go to the wall. The law of the jungle is not the law of civilisation. Humans came of age, he argued, when they ceased emulating nature. He was correct. Nevertheless the contention has often been challenged, not least by his grandson Julian Huxley who gave the Romanes Lecture fifty years later under the same title, 'Evolution and Ethics'. He contended that our task was to find out the direction of evolution and promote the ongoing natural stream. He was wrong. Away back in 1633 John Donne challenged the idea of nature as our guide in an essay entitled 'Nature Our Worst Guide'. So far as our behaviour is concerned, he was correct.

Ethics concerns values and their justification in terms of what contributes most to the richness of life of all peoples and other creatures who share the Earth with us. If we need to turn to biology it would be to find out how what we have inherited in terms of genes and environment can be used or changed to the best social advantage. For example, a responsible society will be deeply opposed to weapons of mass destruction and their possible deleterious effects on both genes and environment. A society is judged, not by how it helps the fit to survive but by how it deals with the marginalised and oppressed. The World Council of Churches has this as a social priority which it expresses in somewhat archaic language 'that God has a preferential option for the poor'. So should we.

What one believes about human nature determines the sort of society we create. There is a perpetual memorial to this reality in a villa on the shores of lake Grossen Wannsee in Berlin. Nos 56–8 Am Grossen Wannsee is an elegant villa in an elegant suburb. There on 20 January 1942 Reinhard Heydrich, then aged thirty-seven, determined the detailed plans for the 'Final Solution'. Heydrich's assistant at the meeting was Adolf Eichmann, just two years his junior. The meeting brought together representatives of the two centres of power in Nazi Germany, the Reich Security Main Office and the German Government. According to the official notes of the conference, found many decades later, Heydrich called the meeting in his capacity as 'Plenipotentiary for the Preparation of the Final Solution of the European Jewish Question'. Heydrich explained that the 'final solution' concerned not only those Jews already under German rule, but some 11 million Jews throughout Europe. He gave the Gestapo chief who attended a list of the numbers involved. The largest number were 2,994,684 Jews in the Ukraine; the next largest group was 2,284,000 Jews in Poland. Anyone visiting the villa, now a memorial, can see the total lists of the numbers of Jews in each country who were to be disposed of. It was numbers that counted, not individuals. It was a logistical problem that the meeting had to solve: how to evict Jews from their homes, how to transport them great distances during wartime to concentration camps, how to separate those who could be useful in labour camps from those who had to be disposed of immediately on arrival at extermination camps such as Birkenau in Poland. Listening inside the villa to the statistics of those marked out for death were a dozen German civil servants. Eight of them had university doctorates. Heydrich told them that they were involved in a 'natural selection' for the good of the nation. At his trial in Jerusalem Eichmann talked of the proceedings in a matter-of-fact way. There was a job to be done and they did it. It took just one day and at the end of that day, he said, they spent time relaxing together (Gilbert 1997).

In the Nazi version of human nature, individuals were not valued for what they were but for how they contributed to the state. To achieve the pure Nazi state there would have to be a severe 'natural selection' to get rid of the unwanted who included, besides Jews, gipsies and homosexuals. All would be labelled and treated as statistics. The bureaucrats who did the 'natural selection' were in many cases highly intelligent, eager young people. They were loyal and knew to

whom they had to be loyal. No doubt some of them would have pre-
ferred to serve other values but to do so could mean sudden death in
a state which required loyalty above all else. By contrast, a democratic state is built on the proposition that all individuals have equality
of opportunity to develop their talents and fulfil their lives. There can
be no discrimination of particular groups in that society but there has
to be freedom of expression and opportunity for persuasion. The
structure of politics in a democratic society should be such as to bring
these values to the top. It will happen to the extent to which the people have a belief in human nature that is fulfilling. It does matter what
we think about human nature. The word democracy comes from the
Greek *demos* (people) and *kratia* (authority), hence 'rule by the people'. Since the Greeks first introduced democracy in many states in
the fifth century BC there has been disagreement as to what constitutes the essential elements of democracy. The debate still goes on.
Its various forms are forever on trial. And that is how it should be.

RACE

All people, be they black, white or yellow in their skin colour belong
to the one species *Homo sapiens.* We all have the one humanity.
Moreover, the more we know about what at one time were called
human races we find that variation within a 'race' in any particular
characteristic is greater than variation between so-called races. The
more we know the less possible it is to separate so-called races, except
in the most superficial characteristics such as skin colour. It is not
possible, for example, to separate so-called races in terms of blood
groups. Some individuals are type B, some type A. some type AB and
some O. No human population is exclusively of one blood type. The
differences between African, Asian and European populations is only
in the proportion of the four kinds. No single individual can be
regarded as a typical member of a race. So it would be incorrect to
say that this particular African and this particular European are different races because of blood group. When a large number of genes
for blood groups are studied in different 'races' such as people from
Africa and those from Europe, the difference between these populations is very small compared with the genetic variation among individuals of any group. Racial differentiation is skin deep only.

This biological finding is very important to understand, especially
for people who live in multicultural societies such as Australia and the
USA. There are cultural differences between people brought up in
East Asia and say those brought up in England. But these differences
iron out in a newly adopted culture within a generation, except when
there has been a deliberate and doubtless praiseworthy attempt to

preserve some cultural values such as music and dance. We know much more on this subject now than we did in the 1930s when Hitler established his racial and eugenic laws that began with the sterilisation of the mentally unfit, the 'morally undesirable' and ended in the extermination of Jews with others in Auschwitz. The claims of genetic determinists in Nazi Germany to scientific respectability led to the gas chambers and the 'Final Solution'. It is deeply regrettable that today what biologists know on the subject of race has had little effect on the everyday consciousness that many people have about race.

Many lay people would describe Australian Aborigines as backward. Australia is the sole continent where in modern times all native peoples still lived without any of the hallmarks of so-called civilisation—without farming, herding, metal, buildings or writing. They were nomadic hunter-gatherers. During the last thousand or more decades less cultural change has taken place amongst Australian Aborigines than amongst peoples in any other continent. Yet as of 40,000 years ago Australian Aborigines enjoyed a head start over societies elsewhere, so why did they not develop a civilisation as many other societies eventually did? The simple answer is a supposed biological difference. Wrong! Jared Diamond (1998) has shown that the differences cannot be laid at the door of race or inherent features of the people themselves. The inequality stems instead from the availability of resources on the different continents. Australia had no domesticable native animals. The sole foreign domesticated animal adopted in Australia was the dog, which arrived from Asia around 1500 BC and established itself to become the dingo. Agriculture was another non-starter in Australia. Australia is not only the driest inhabited continent but also the one with the most infertile soils. Furthermore, Australia has a paucity of domesticable wild plants. Even modern European geneticists have failed to develop any crop except macadamia nuts from the Australian flora. The Aboriginal substitute for food production has been termed 'firestick farming'. This is the intentional burning of the countryside. It made it easier to catch the animals and the fires stimulated the growth of new vegetation.

Why did Australian Aborigines not develop metal tools, writing and complex societies? Diamond argues that they remained hunter-gathers whereas these further developments arose only in people who were numerous and were food producers. How can we account for the fact that white English colonists just over two centuries ago created a literate, food-producing, industrial society within a few decades of colonisation? The resolution of the problem is simple. White English colonists did not create a literate, food-producing industrial society. They imported all the elements from outside

Australia, the livestock, all the crops (except macadamia nuts), steam engines, guns, the alphabet and political institutions. All these were the end products of 10,000 years of development in Eurasia. Europeans have never learned to survive in Australia without their inherited technology, as the fate of early explorers demonstrated. The Australian Aborigine is one of a number of examples which Jared Diamond has investigated in great detail, all of which show how the differences between cultures is primarily environmental and not genetic.

AUGUSTINE, PELAGIUS AND CHRYSOSTOM

In the dialogue the *Phaedrus* Plato figures the human soul as a charioteer, struggling with an unruly horse, his animal nature, but struggling also to recall and retain the vision of truth, temperance, justice and beauty which he saw before birth when he drove across the heaven in the company of the gods. Often the struggle ended in defeat. But the greatest Greeks did succeed in reining in these rebellious horses. Richard Livingstone (1915), a philosopher of the ancient Greeks, suspects that Plato was like many of his colleagues a man of violent passions who only reached freedom after a long struggle. That was in the fourth century BC.

Is there a beast wrestling with an angel in each of us? That is the question three theologians of the fourth century CE wrestled with. One of them, Augustine of Hippo, had a problem. He was a genetic determinist. He was born in North Africa in 354 CE and became a nominal Christian. In the biblical story of creation, where his predecessors for centuries had found a message of freedom, Augustine came to read a story of human bondage from original sin. Humanity is sick, suffering and helpless, irreparably damaged by the Fall. We are ridden with guilt. Augustine tried to understand the turbulent experience of his own life, especially the occasions of sexual desire and of grief. Given his intense inner conflicts and his passionate nature and the struggle to control his sexual impulses which he reveals in his *Confessions*, he abandoned the belief of his predecessors in free will and the power to control oneself. He could not acknowledge these qualities as a reality in his life or even a genuine good in his experience, let alone in the rest of humanity. Describing in his *Confessions* his struggle to be chaste, Augustine recalls how, 'in the sixteenth year of the age of my flesh ... the madness of raging lust exercised its supreme domination over me'. Through sexual desire, he says, ' my enemy trod me down and seduced me'. Of his sexual involvements he admitted that 'I drew my shackles along with me terrified to have them knocked off'. Commenting that one of his friends was 'amazed at my enslavement', Augustine reflects 'what made me a slave to it was the habit of insatiable lust'. He had a problem all right.

Wherein lay Augustine's problem? It was, he claimed, inherent. After Adam sinned his punishment was a punishment of the whole human race—in effect a genetic mutation that was to burden all his offspring for all subsequent history. Augustine derived this theory from his own peculiar interpretation of Romans 5:12: 'Through one man sin entered the world'. That sin consisted of uncontrolled libido. The problem, said Augustine, was 'the nature of the semen from which we were propagated'. That semen transmits the shackles that bind us. Hence Augustine concludes that every human being ever conceived through semen is born contaminated by sin, not just from birth but from the moment of conception. The whole of the human race is contaminated except for Christ, born without libido because conceived without semen. Hence away back in the fourth century Augustine elaborated this complex argument for genetic determinism. It did not go unchallenged.

Born about the same time as Augustine was John Chrysostom of Antioch, acknowledged as the greatest preacher of the ancient church and aptly called the golden tongued. He recognised the role of imperial rule as being necessary because of human sin of individuals, families and whole societies. The role of the external government is to keep that under control and it did so successfully, more or less. That coercive role of the state contrasts sharply with the liberty enjoyed by an inner self-rule of those who have discovered the liberation of the Christian faith. Chrysostom proclaimed human freedom, the opposite of Augustine's claim, and saw human nature as having within it the capacity for both good and evil. The task of the church was to persuade its followers to pursue the good.

Chrysostom was not alone. A contemporary British monk, Pelagius, considered as crucial a text in Matthew from the Sermon on the Mount: 'Be ye perfect, even as your Father which is in heaven is perfect'. Pelagius proclaimed that Jesus laid it down that men and women are to be perfect themselves. Jesus would hardly have made such a claim or command for us to become something we are incapable of becoming. It follows that humans must be able to become perfect themselves (Passmore 1970). Everything good and everything evil, Pelagius argued, is not born with us but done by us. We are born with a capacity for either sort of living. Men are born with a capacity for evil but also with a capacity for perfecting themselves by the exercise of their free will. Sin is a matter of bad habits. An immediate effect of Pelagianism was to provoke Augustine to write a long series of anti-Pelaginan tracts.

Augustine was finally to be the victor. In 529 CE the Council of Orange used Augustine's own words to assert that original sin corrupted the whole human race. It rejected the view that men are free to choose good or evil. Pelagius was declared a heretic by councils in 416 CE and 418 CE. He was excommunicated and banished from Rome. Chrysostom got off rather lightly. He rose to a pinnacle of ecclesiastical power by being appointed bishop of Constantinople, which ranked second only to the bishop of Rome. However, his acts of social conscience for the benefit of the marginalised and oppressed turned people against him. He was expelled from office and died in exile a few years later. Passmore (1970) sees the history of Christianity as a long controversy in which Christians swung between the extremes of Pelagianism and Augustinian belief. Within the Christian churches today there is a spectrum of belief from Pelagianism to Augustianism with Augustine probably in the ascendancy.

Augustine's argument had serious implications for the authority of both church and state which he was at pains to point out. For the Catholic Church to yield to Pelagianism, he claimed, would be for the church to lose its vast authority as the only force that could liberate men from themselves. By insisting that humanity ravaged by sin lay helplessly in need of external intervention, Augustine's theory not only justified the imposition of church authority but also validated its imperial patrons with their secular power, all for the ends of human salvation. Just how humans were to be released from the shackles of inborn sin presented problems for the Augustinians. Augustine himself changed his views on this more than once. But he seemed to imply that salvation did not come primarily through human effort but through the external intervention of God, a sort of divine therapy replacing the mutant gene with a good one!

Elaine Pagels (1988), whose analysis I have mostly followed, considers that the surviving influence of Augustine for a millennium and a half to our own day was in part due to the way his view forged the uneasy alliance between the Catholic churches and imperial power and justified this alliance for the majority of Christians.

As for the reformers, Luther was totally against Pelagianism and so was Calvin, though Reinhold Niebuhr considered that Calvin got close to Pelagianism by allowing too much sanctity and righteousness by overemphasis on sensual sin which men can learn to control rather than the more fundamental sin of pride (Passmore 1970 p. 111). Calvin was the arch-genetic determinist of all theologians. The destiny of each individual was determined at birth. Everyone is born a sinner but some lucky ones, the elect, are predestined by God for eternal life. The unelect are destined to eternal death. But no-one knows who are the chosen ones.

All who think are to some extent stretched out on the Procrustean bed that would cut us down to size. But we can jump out of that fate and work out or own salvation even though it might well be with fear and trembling.

Peter Singer (1998) approaches these problems not from the perspective of religion but as a non-religious ethicist. He attributes a large part of the failure of socialist movements of the twentieth century to an unrealistic dream of the perfectibility of humankind. Instead he urges that we accept as realities certain aspects of human nature that tend to militate against perfectibility and deal with them. Some of these realities he urges us to be realistic about are:

- Accept that there is such a thing as human nature and seek to find out more about it.
- Reject any implication that from what is can be derived what ought to be.
- Accept the competitive spirit of human beings under quite different economic conditions.
- Expect people to respond positively to invitations to cooperate for mutual benefit and promote structures in society that will move in that direction.
- Recognise that the exploitation of non-humans is a legacy of a past which did not appreciate the inner lives of non-humans and work toward the higher moral status of non-humans.
- Be on the side of the weak, poor and oppressed.

Perhaps more than any one else in this century, Reinhold Niebuhr recognised and articulated an incongruity in our natures which creates a fundamental human problem. Neither our nature nor culture is bad. One problem of locating evil either within nature or culture is that it makes the human problem something outside the human will. It is too easy for us to say we are victims of our genes or victims of our environment, or spectators of others who are regarded as such victims. Niebuhr addresses us in terms of our responsibility. It is not the situation in which we find ourselves but what we freely do in it that is the basic evil. For example, the admirable will to live fully is transmuted into the desire for power and glory. The urge to live fully becomes transmuted by overweening self-interest into a will to power over others. It leads to destructive competition for a place in the sun. Niebuhr may well have agreed with Singer's diagnosis that the left political movements placed too much confidence on the perfectibility of humankind. But he would have been less sanguine than Singer in the extent to which self-interest can be restrained in the interest of the common good.

Speaking at the grave of Galina Starovoitova, after she was murdered in St Petersburg, one of the mourners said: 'No-one among us expected that the road to freedom would be so difficult'. Writing about this tragic occasion, Adam Michnik (1999) said that freedom is for everybody—also for cheaters and hooligans. When freedom is young it is accompanied by an undeclared war between the idealist and the gangster. Galina fell victim in such a war. Freedom was born with a new hope with the new general secretary Mikhail Gorbachev who came with the three words: *perestroika, uskorenie, glasnost*—reconstruction, speeding up, transparency. These words provoked fright, distrust and hope. The fright was for men in the *apparat*, whose seats were shaking beneath them. The distrust was among the hardened emigrés who saw in them a shrewd move by the communist power. Hope was awakened among the intelligence. Gala Starovoitova was among the first to place their faith in hope. So did Dmitriyevich Sakharov, the great physicist. They met regularly in a club to discuss issues facing the nation. But everyday life became very difficult with unemployment, poverty, criminal scandals and corruption. The people felt lost among empty words and the fear of tomorrow. The democrats among them slipped into quarrels, conflicts and plots. And when the first leader of change, Gorbachev, contended the presidency he received less than 1 per cent of the vote. In his analysis Michnik concluded: 'There are people who live in order to kill. Such are Galina's assassins and their masters. And there are people who live to help others to live, and the are sometimes killed because of that. Galina Starovoitova was such a person' (p. 6).

At the opening of a new sitting of the South African parliament in Cape Town on February 1999 Nelson Mandela called for a 'reconstruction and development programme [RDP] of the soul'. RDP is one of the strategies the Mandela government introduced to rebuild the nation. 'Our first task,' said Mandela, 'is to change and improve the basic living conditions for people, through the provision of houses, clean water, electricity, health care, education, security and protection.' He went on to say that they were learning every day that there is an even more basic task of reconstruction if they are to make their country genuinely reconstructed. It is the task of moral reconstruction. 'Quite clearly,' said the president, 'there is something wrong with a society where freedom is interpreted to mean that teachers or students get to school drunk; warders chase away management and appoint their own friends to lead institutions; striking workers resort to violence and destruction of property; business people lavish money on court cases simply to delay implementation of legislation they do not like; and tax evasion turns individuals into heroes at dinner-table talk. Something drastic needs to be done about this' (Bruyns 1999). Nor is Mandela alone in so thinking.

In his presidential state of the republic address to the parliament and senate of the Czech Republic, Vaclev Havel (1998) stressed his longstanding belief in the importance of the institutions of civil society to channel human nature into creative activities for the common good. He declared that the ideal of success and profit in the republic was defiled because the state of affairs permitted the most immoral to become the most successful and the greatest profits to be made by thieves who stole with impunity. Under the cloak of an unqualified liberalism, morality, decency, humility before the order of nature, concern for future generations, respect for law, the culture of interpersonal relationships—all were trivialised as icing on the cake of the forces of economic production. He went on to say that, drunk with power and success, a blind eye was turned to one thing after another until eventually scandals had become widespread in the very central and proud activity of the new republic—privatisation. People had forgotten, he said, that people by their nature have inner needs to work for the common good. This had been superseded by hubris and selfishness. Havel pleaded for the parliament and senate to say clearly to their fellow citizens that real humanity and real prosperity are unthinkable without clear, good and widely understood and respected rules to govern the various areas of life. And that is the kernel of the problem, our problem, how to channel creativity and curb its opposite. Havel was speaking out from the experience of oppression from the Nazis, then from an imposed socialist government and more latterly from a society that knew freedom but did not know what to do with it. His agony comes through his words. Would that more of our political leaders had such a vision and identified the human pitfalls in a free society.

Reinhold Niebuhr (1966) emphasised that an adequate political ethic is not established merely by conceiving the most ideal possible solution to political problems. It must deal with the realities of human nature, as well as the ideal possibilities. It must recognise the difficulty which all of us find in conforming our actions to our highest ideals. 'It is very difficult,' said Niebuhr, 'to establish peaceful and just communities, because the collective behaviour of mankind is even more egotistic than individual behaviour' (p. 30). Our job is therefore to establish a tolerable community within the limits set by human recalcitrance. At a time when the Graeco–Roman civilisation was relapsing into the Dark Ages, St Augustine published his *De Civitate Dei*—the Commonwealth of God. It was an attempt to provide ethical and political principles for a better world. In more recent times Lionel Curtis (1938), identifying the '30s as a period in which human affairs were descending into chaos, wrote his monumental work *The Commonwealth of God* to do for his generation what Augustine had done for his. The time is ripe to do this again for the new millennium.

This chapter has dealt with some key human issues to do with human nature. The next chapter deals the nature of nature that includes all life.

5

ROMANCING NATURE

When flowers bloom on concrete life has triumphed.

Berlin Wall graffiti

The previous chapter was concerned with the nature of human nature. In this chapter we concern ourselves with the nature of nature, that is to say the ecological world. We raise the question as to the conditions that make survival of life of millions of species on this Earth possible, how many fall by the wayside and how we can support the lives of those creatures on which we depend for our own lives. Our lives are utterly dependent upon the resources and services that nature provides. So a minimum requirement of our relationship to nature is that we sustain the viability of those resources and services. Our quality of life is dependent upon the quality and quantity of these resources and services. A second less acknowledged requirement is that we recognise the intrinsic value of creatures other than ourselves which inhabit the Earth with us whether they are necessary for our lives or not. We are not the only pebbles on the cosmic beach. These others have rights too.

The ecological crisis has brought with it two responses. One is a deeper scientific understanding of ecology and our place in the natural scheme of things. Secondly it has brought to the fore a certain romantic view of nature which tends to be emphasised by the media. It is a view also of some environmentalists. The romantic view tends to emphasise wholeness, unity, connectedness, fragility and the idea that any interference of any part of an ecological community will upset the whole and lead to disorder and chaos. The truth is rather different. Life is a struggle against enormous odds and seems ever to have been so. Any ecologist who has studied plants and animals in nature knows this. I shall never forget what seemed to me at the time a triumph of nature to see flowers blooming of their own accord in the war ruins around St Paul's Cathedral in London in 1947. Today we see it in ruins that are left in Berlin. There are both facts and fables in our present view of nature and its ecology. Here are some of the fables of which we ask: is this good science? The chapter concludes with a workmanlike approach to nature and our role in it.

THE BALANCE OF NATURE MYTH

That there is a balance of nature is widely held by people who think at all about nature. It is the idea that organisms in a community such as a forest or a lake are automatically harmoniously adjusted to one another so that a state of equilibrium exists. It includes the notion that significant changes in numbers of a species occur only when something upsets the natural 'balance'. It is a view that is perpetuated in popular magazines and some nature films and so has become part of the lore of the man in the street. It is a view which has persisted in the minds of some environmentalists and professional ecologists. After all, you can go back day after day or year after year to your favourite forest or lake and nothing much seems to have changed. Nothing is further from the truth. The truth is that change, not stability, is the rule.

In some form or other the concept of balance has been hotly disputed by ecologists over the past fifty years or so. Some have maintained that the concept is still relevant, while others deny that any balance of nature exists. The present trend is against balance. The historian of ecology Donald Worster (1997) writes: 'Over the past two decades the field of ecology has pretty well demolished Eugene Odum's portrayal of a world of ecosystems tending toward equilibrium' (p. 72). Likewise population ecologists Picket and White (1985) point out that until the 1980s the major priority of research in both theoretical and empirical work in ecology was dominated by the equilibrium perspective. Repudiating that perspective and embracing one of constant change, these authors examine the evidence for equilibrium or otherwise in what have been regarded until recently as examples of equilibrium, namely tropical rainforests of South and Central America and the watery Everglades of Florida. They find instabilities on every hand; a wet green world of constant disturbance and changing patchiness. The message is consistent. The old concept of equilibrium is dead and with it the overused concept of the ecosystem has receded in usefulness. In its place nature is a landscape of patchiness, changing through space and time, with an increasing barrage of perturbations and change. Life is struggle.

In 1967 Paul Ehrlich and I wrote a paper giving arguments against the concept of balance of nature (Birch & Ehrlich 1967). We maintain that the arguments in that paper remain valid. Adelaide ecologist H. G. Andrewartha and I wrote two books putting an alternative model to the balance of nature concept (Andrewartha & Birch 1954, 1984). We were in a minority when we wrote but that may not be the case now. We regarded our joint project as very important, for it made all the difference as to how one studied nature. We were population ecologists. Others were community ecologists. Recently Paul Ehrlich (1997) has written against the balance of nature concept. 'We are,' he says, 'properly nervous about having our science distorted— of seeing pronouncements by environmentalists, such as "Complexity enhances stability" or references to "balance of nature" that do not necessarily reflect a current disciplinary consensus' (p. 6).

Another population biologist Richard Lewontin (1991) of Harvard University writes:

> The banner of 'save the Environment' ... assumes that there is such a thing as the balance of nature, that everything is in a balance or harmony that is being destroyed only by the foolishness and greed of humans. There is nothing in our knowledge of the world to suggest that there is any particular balance or harmony. The physical and biological worlds since the beginning of the earth have been in constant state of flux and change, much of which has been far more drastic than anyone can now conceive. (p. 118)

The Permian extinction of about 250 million years ago wiped out 90 percent of all species on Earth. Some 65 million years ago the dinosaurs, which were widespread over the face of the Earth, were wiped out, seemingly by the impact of an asteroid. A succession of ice ages changed the face of nature on all continents. In the last ice age slabs of ice stretched as far south as London and New York. That was some 20,000 years ago. A hundred thousand years ago the conditions were similar to today. Some 20,000 years before that another big freeze had come over the Earth. This drastic change from cold to warm to cold has been going on for the past million years.

There has never been a balance or harmony. During both the cold and the warm phases countless species found themselves unadapted and became extinct. Fully 99.999 per cent of all species that have ever existed are already extinct. Ultimately this is the fate of all species. In the process of evolution there are far more losers than winners. Life is now about half over. The first living organisms appeared on Earth about 3 to 4 billion years ago. Cosmologists promise us another 3 to 4 billion years before everything comes to an end. Considering such a history, Lewontin (1991) concludes that 'any rational environmental movement must abandon the romantic and totally unfounded ideological commitment to a harmonious and balanced world in which the environment is preserved' (p. 119).

Michael Soule (1995) is another population biologist who, in recent times, has argued strongly against the concept of balance of nature. He writes:

> Living nature is not equilibrial, at least not on a scale relevant to the persistence of species. In a sense the science of ecology had been hoist on its own petard by maintaining, as many did during the middle of this century, that natural communities tend toward equilibrium. Current ecological thinking argues that nature at the level of biotic assemblages has never been homeostatic. (p. 143)

Indeed the word *never* would seem to apply the absence of balance right from the birth of life itself on Earth. Such now seems to be the case. Until recently students of the origin of life imagined that life might have begun in some warm and shallow tropical sea because it was there that it seemed most likely a soup of organic molecules might be synthesised leading on to the first living cells. But such a Garden of Eden is now believed to be a bit of a myth. From the fossil record we can deduce that life was flourishing 3.5 billion years ago and quite possibly nearly 4 billion years ago. In his book on life's origin Paul Davies (1998) gives a graphic picture of what early life must have had to contend with. Both Earth and Moon endured a punishing cosmic barrage until 3.8 million years ago. All the bodies in the inner solar system were bombarded by asteroids and giant comets coming in from the outer solar system. The ferocity was very great between 4 and 3.8 million years ago. The larger collisions during a heavy bombardment must have stripped away much of the atmosphere and oceans. The scale of the impact would have been far worse than the impact that caused the annihilation of the dinosaurs 65 million years ago. As late as 3.8 billon years ago the Moon was hit by an object 90 kilometres in diameter, producing a colossal impact basin much bigger than the size of the British Isles. Earth must have suffered cataclysms of similar magnitude. On a huge impact the surface temperature of the impacted Earth might have soared to 3000 degrees C, causing all the world's oceans to boil dry and melting rock to a depth of a kilometre. Davies points out that such impacts would have thoroughly sterilised the

surface of the Earth, perhaps for thousands of years. If life had originated on the surface of Earth it must have been annihilated and perhaps started all over again on the return of less hostile conditions.
This might have been after a period of 200 million years or so. Life
might have arisen at any time after about 4 billion years ago, flour-
ished but only to be wiped out by the next sterilising impact. Davies
(1998) summarises the situation thus:

> From what we know of the early history of the solar system, the
> Earth's surface was a hazardous place for a living organism to be for at
> least several hundred million years. Even the bottom of the ocean
> would afford little protection against the violence of the larger
> impactors. The heat pulses from these cataclysms would have been
> lethal to a depth of tens or even hundreds of metres into the Earth's
> crust itself. Hardly a Garden of Eden! (p. 127)

This leads to the proposal that life may have originated (or survived after originating elsewhere) from a half to one kilometre or
even more below the surface of the Earth, where today many bacteria thrive in what for most organisms would be extremely hostile
conditions. They live, not by photosynthesis (as green plants do), but
by chemosynthesis. Commonly they metabolise sulphur which is in
abundance. It would not be too far out to say they eat sulphur at
temperatures well over 100 degrees C. Hence Davies speaks of the
rise of life as 'Ascent from Hades'. Such a story hardly bespeaks of a
universe friendly to life. Yet in another context, which we discuss in
chapter 6, the universe can be conceived as bio-friendly, as indeed
Davies himself (1998) concludes.

So life's beginning was no Garden of Eden! There is no balance
of nature and never has been. Yet life survives. And so do we, but it
is a struggle! With what then do we replace the balance of nature?
The full answer is complex because nature is complex. An alternative
vision sees a much more chaotic state in nature than balance suggests.
In fact this alternative theory has been called a chaos theory of
nature. It looks as though each species in a community of plants and
animals has a particular probability of surviving and reproducing.
That may be quite low for some species, in which case the species
becomes rare. For others the chance is high, which could lead to
'outbreaks' in numbers to huge levels such as is a regular phenomenon in locusts and plague grasshoppers. A species may be kept rare
or common by any component of its environment that affects its
chance to survive and reproduce. This is what the study of ecology is
all about. Ecologists ask the question: how is it that lions do not

cause their prey such as antelopes to become extinct, or why don't wolves on Isle Royale National Park, an island in Lake Michigan, cause moose, on which they prey, to become extinct? Well they do in some localities. Contrary to traditional notions, there is no simple 'balance' relationship between a predator and its prey but a combination of many factors that lead in many localities to the survival of both, yet in anything but a balanced state. Within the habitat there are enclaves where the prey and predator survive. In other enclaves predator, prey or both become extinct.

Ecologists agree on many things. Virtually without exception they agree that there is an environmental crisis created by humans. It is not a case of humans upsetting some mystical balance but in general it is simply a case of destruction of habitats. As yet there is no grand unified theory of ecology that has a consensus. There are schools of thought that tend to change with time. Much more is to be known than at present is know.

ARE ECOSYSTEMS FRAGILE?

Environmentalists who set out to save a coral reef threatened by human activities are tempted to argue with developers that coral reefs are fragile ecosystems. They infer that if you disturb any one part of the system the whole collapses. But as Ehrlich (1997) says: 'It is rare that any ecosystem can usefully be described as "fragile" ... That wetlands and tropical forests are rapidly disappearing is beyond dispute; whether or not they are normally "fragile" is beside the point' (p. 101). Fragility is an example of an outdated concept that can backfire against well-intentioned greens who invoke it for support against developers.

The word ecosystem is itself a metaphor. People refer to a lake as an ecosystem or a coral reef as an ecosystem, quite often implying that these communities are mathematically structured like some sort of computer system. The term is meant to include all plants, animals and micro-organisms together with the water and nutrients. A problem with the concept is that boundaries are not easy to define. A bird that flies over a lake yet leaves its droppings in the make may have some effect on the organisms in the lake. But it may live kilometres away. So where does the lake's ecosystem end? The concept is an abstraction from nature.

Ecologists are divided amongst themselves as to the best way to study ecology. There are those who say let us study the lake and everything in it. They might come up with a huge inventory of organisms and minerals and what have you. They are community ecologists. There are others who say: let us study the fish in the lake and what determines their chance to survive and reproduce. They are population ecologists. They may well claim that they have more chance of getting answers to questions than the community ecologists, who might find it difficult to be clear as to what the important questions are. They will tell us that it is complicated and will draw up complex circular diagrams of food chains and other relationships. But even they are unlikely to say that this or that ecosystem is fragile.

IS NATURE BENIGN AND HARMONIOUS?

The natural theology of the late eighteenth century saw in the order of nature a perfect design of plants and animals. In many cases the design was seen as directed to human ends. The bee collected nectar not for itself but to make honey for us. The designer was God. There was something perfect about nature.

In 1859 Darwin told a very different story in *The Origin of Species*. It contrasts with the design argument in three respects:

- Nature is not complete and perfect. It is still in process of being made and always has been.
- The process involves chance rather than design.
- Nature is a vast struggle for existence.

It was this third aspect of Darwinism which struck at the notion of nature as benign and harmonious. Nine years before the publication of *The Origin of Species* Tennyson had already described nature as 'red in tooth and claw'. And well before that William Blake asked of the tiger, 'Did he who made the Lamb make thee?' Thomas Henry Huxley said nature was 'a gigantic gladiatorial show'. G. J. Romanes (1848–94), an Oxford professor, specialist in animal psychology and enthusiastic supporter of Darwin, said after millions of years of evolution 'we find that more than half of the species which have survived the ceaseless struggle are parasitic in their habits, lower and insentient forms of life feasting on higher and sentient forms; we find teeth and talons whetted for slaughter, hooks and suckers moulded for torment—everywhere a reign of terror, hunger, and sickness, with oozing blood and quivering limbs, with gasping breath and eyes of innocence that dimly close in deaths of brutal torture!' (Passmore 1970 p. 245). Struggle is indeed one aspect of nature. Lions hunt and kill antelopes. Wasps hunt caterpillars into which they lay their eggs so that the wasp larvae survive at the expense of caterpillars. As a whole, more individuals are born into the world of nature than can possibly survive. This is particularly obvious with plants and marine animals.

Darwin (1859) devoted a whole chapter in *The Origin of Species* to the struggle for existence—a phrase he borrowed from Thomas Malthus' 'Essay on Population'. He made it clear that the phrase was a metaphor. It included much more than predation of one organism on another. Darwin wrote:

> Two canine animals in time of dearth, may be truly said to struggle with each other who shall get food and live. A plant on the edge of a desert is said to struggle for life against drought, though more properly it should be said to be dependent upon moisture. A plant which annually produces a thousand seeds, for which only one on the average came to maturity, may be more truly said to struggle with the plants of the same and other kinds which already clothe the ground. (Darwin 1859; 1901 ed. p. 58)

Darwin saw the struggle for existence going on between an individual organism and any component of its environment such as temperature, moisture, other individuals of the same kind and others of different kinds such as predators. Many are called but few are chosen. In contemplating this scene in nature, Whitehead (1929a) said: 'But whether or no it be for the general good, life is robbery' (p. 105). He added the metaphysical comment: 'It is at this point that with life morals become acute. The robber requires justification.'

Darwin was fully aware that plants and animals also had relations that were cooperative, such as bees that pollinate plants, yet none escapes its own struggle for existence. Population biologist Michael Soule (1995) made a timely criticism of worn-out views of ecology parading as modern ecology when he wrote:

> The real biological world little resembles the rose-tinted television portrayal. Certainly the idea that species live in integrated communities is a myth. So-called biotic communities, a misleading term, are constantly changing membership. The species occurring in an any particular place are rarely convivial neighbours; their co-existence in certain places is better explained by individual physiological tolerances ... Though in some cases the finer details of spatial distribution may be influenced by positive interspecies interactions, the much more common kinds of interactions are competition, predation, parasitism and disease ... The idea that living nature comprises co-operative communities replete with altruistic, mutualistic symbiosis has been overstated. (p. 143)

IS NATURE COMPLETED AND FINE-TUNED?

As discussed in the previous section, nature is ever changing both in numbers of individuals and in numbers of species. In another sense also it is incomplete and changing. This is because the creative process of evolution, by which all creatures come into existence and stay in existence, is always going on. It never finishes. Central to the process of evolution is the continuous production of mutant genes, most of which are deleterious. But some few add to the adaptiveness of the species and are incorporated into their genetic composition.

It is now known that genes that confer on insects resistance to insecticides such as DDT were being produced even before DDT existed. They did not persist in the population then because they did not confer any added advantage until DDT arrived on the scene. This happened when DDT was invented by chemists and used as an insecticide. DDT-resistant mutants, which were wiped out before DDT became part of the insect's environment, now survived in preference to those without the mutant gene. Central to the process is the idea of chance variation and the selection of those variants that confer benefit on the species. It is an order of nature very different from that of a design made by an external omnipotent deity, a view common in Darwin's day.

After Darwin we have to take seriously a role of chance in the creative process and the fact that evolution goes on without ceasing. Nature is incomplete and is tied up with a hit-and-miss process, mostly miss. The amazing thing is that the potentiality for change in a chance process of mutation for every species is virtually infinite by virtue of the complex nature of the gene and its capacity to change. Even now gene mutations are being produced that could confer resistance to some future poison agent that chemists have not yet invented. It would be true to say that nature is profligate, both in this respect and because of the huge numbers of individuals of most species born into the world.

DOES COMPLEXITY ENHANCE STABILITY?

A much contested proposition amongst ecologists is the thesis that diversity of species in a community enhances stability in the sense that the number of individuals and the number of species in the community are kept more or less constant. There is so much dispute amongst ecologists, based on mathematical models and observations in nature, that it is unwise at this stage to place much credence on this and related propositions. Environmentalists would be wise to base their pleas for biodiversity on other grounds, of which there are a number.

Richard Levins and Richard Lewontin are two leading evolutionists who maintain that virtually all modern theorist of evolution, especially evolutionary ecologists, have claimed that complexity results in stability. It has been supposed that a community with many different predators, competitors, decomposers and primary food sources is the most resistant to change. Hence the proposition that evolution leads to greater and greater diversity, complexity, home-ostasis and stability in the living world. However, it is wise to heed what Levins and Lewontin (1985) say about this thesis: 'The extra-ordinary feature of this conceptual structure is that it has no appar-ent basis either in fact or in theory' (p. 21).

Whatever we think about stability and complexity, it makes no difference whatsoever to the program of conservation aimed to main-tain biodiversity. There are other arguments for maintaining diversi-ty of species. A cogent one is that diversity of organisms is required to maintain the life-support systems of the Earth. These are the cycles in nature that help to maintain the constancy in composition of the atmosphere, the water cycle and the cycle of nutrients; a diversity of organisms is involved in the detoxification and decomposition of wastes. Ecologists do not know enough about these processes to be able to pinpoint all the organisms that are involved. Our ignorance suggest that a precautionary policy of conservation is the wise path to take. But let us use the right arguments.

Because there is no consensus about the stability–complexity argument, it is inappropriate to include it in an environmental ethic as in Aldo Leopold's so-called land ethic which says 'A thing is right when it tends to promote the integrity, stability and beauty of the biotic community'. Not necessarily so. An environmental ethic needs to be informed by science. What is important is that the science which is taken into account is valid science.

IS THE EARTH A SUPER-ORGANISM?

The idea that the Earth is a self-regulating super-organism was brought to life in 1972 in the so-called Gaia hypothesis of James Lovelock, a distinguished atmospheric chemist. Gaia is the name of the Greek Earth Goddess. The Earth is conceived to be a linked sys-tem of physical, chemical and biological processes interacting in a self-regulating way to maintain the conditions necessary for life. The Gaia hypothesis aroused controversy amongst the scientific commu-nity from its beginning. It has been accused of being poorly defined and impossible to subject to any verification test. Worst of all, Gaia received an extra mystical halo, foreign to its author, when it was adopted by the New Age movement.

What is well established is that there are cycles in nature such as the nitrogen cycle, the phosphorus cycle, the carbon cycle and the water cycle. All involve feedback processes that result in the composition of the atmosphere or of the oceans remaining remarkably constant, except for major interventions by humans such as the increase of carbon dioxide in the atmosphere since the Industrial Revolution. A conservative assessment of the Gaia hypothesis is that most of what is true in it has been known for years, such as the feedback cycles involved in the maintenance of constancy of the composition of the atmosphere and the seas. What is new beyond that is questionable. The Earth is not an organism, not even a super-organism. Gaia is a hazardous model for nature as it can give a false sense of security. If nature is self-regulating it will care for itself. The notion can lead to a theory of conservation known as benign neglect.

THE MYTH OF THE DUALITY OF THE NATURAL AND THE ARTIFICIAL

There is not a continent that has not been invaded by species of plants, animals and micro-organisms that were previously foreign to them. Natural communities, so called, are full of invaders. The most common mammals in the wild in Australia are rabbits, cats, mice and goats, all of which came from Europe. All the mammals in New Zealand are from Australia or Europe. In so far as the invaders have survived and continue to reproduce they are part of the present scene of nature. They are natural, if not pristine.

Probably more ecological studies have been made on invaders than on endemic species because of their economic importance. European rabbits destroy grazing lands in Australia. Australian possums in New Zealand destroy forests. The point is that there may be no such thing as a community of plants and animals in the world today that is without its invaders. And the principles of ecology have been largely worked out on invaders simply because of their economic importance. There is no valid distinction between natural communities and so-called artificial ones. One is as natural as the other. The ecological principles that apply to one apply to the other.

There is no doubt that the communities of plants and animals in Australia today differed from those of 60,000 years ago when Aborigines arrived on that continent. After their arrival it is likely that fires increased in frequency, changing the nature of living communities. It is also possible that Aborigines were involved in the extinction of the mammalian megafauna, hunting it for food. Just over 200 years ago the arrival of European humans in Australia resulted in a whole new set of plants and animals getting a foothold. The subsequent advent of agriculture made enormous changes. Forests gave way to grasslands, rivers were dammed and wetlands were drained. So an ecological historian could give a picture of a changing nature in Australia from 60,000 years ago to today. All of these successive phases should be regarded as natural or else are we to make the silly proposition that Australia today has no natural communities of plants and animals? The truth is that humans are as much a part of an ecological community as are other species. We are part of nature.

THE MYTH THAT INDIGENOUS PEOPLE ARE SUPERIOR CONSERVATIONISTS

It is right and proper that we should learn what we can from indigenous people who have lived with nature far longer than most other human communities. Some of what we learn is positive and constructive. On the other hand indigenous people have been responsible for much devastation of nature. We can learn from that also.

Some tribes of Australian Aborigines kept areas which were for them sacred sites free from hunting. Whatever the purpose, the effect was a conserving of native species in these areas. On the other hand Australian Aborigines have been credited by some with the extinction of the large mammals that once roamed that continent. Some sixty species of large marsupials became extinct after Aborigines arrived in 60,000 or more years ago. Furthermore, the Aborigines' use of fire to aid in hunting caused dramatic changes to huge tracts of country. In those National Parks in Australia under Aboriginal control the inhabitants are free to live off the land as their predecessors did. As a result, according to some reports, some species of animals have become rare in some of these parks.

Some tribes in Papua New Guinea are notable for having practised sustainable agriculture for countless years. On the other hand Diamond (1993) claims that in thirty years of visiting native peoples on the three islands of New Guinea he has failed to come across a single example of indigenous New Guineans showing friendly response to wild animals or consciously managing habitats to enhance wildlife. A consequence has been the depleting or extermination of susceptible species. Diamond seeks to dispel what he sees as a myth of native people as 'environmentally minded paragons of conservation, living in a Golden Age of harmony with nature, in which living things are revered, harvested only as needed and carefully monitored to avoid depletion of breeding stocks' (p. 268).

The role of the American Indian in nature has been widely discussed and remains controversial (Nabham 1997). At the end of the Pleistocene epoch 12,000 years ago, about two-thirds of the large mammal species in North America became extinct. Included were several species of large mammoths, giant ground sloths and sabre-toothed cats. Similar losses of large mammals occurred on other continents. The dates of these extinctions more or less coincided with the arrival of humans in the Western Hemisphere. This has led to the theory of Pleistocene overkill. The idea is that the relative poverty today of the Earth's megafauna (animals weighing over 500 kilograms) is due primarily to overexploitation of relatively defenceless large animals by ever-increasing numbers of skilful hunters. Various lines of evidence make it seem likely that human beings got an early start in the process of extinction (Ehrlich & Ehrlich 1981 pp. 109–16). Biologists generally agree that, on the land at least, species are vanishing at a rate of one hundred to a thousand times faster than before the arrival of *Homo sapiens*.

THE FALLACY OF DERIVING ETHICS FROM NATURE

The great protagonist of Darwinism, Thomas Henry Huxley, was deeply concerned that Darwinism, with its concept of struggle for existence and survival of the fittest, might be converted into a social doctrine, as indeed it was by some who saw in the struggle for existence a doctrine to apply to human behaviour. Social Darwinism has been used to support economic and political competition in the belief that this will lead to the survival and increase of the best and strongest. Social Darwinism appealed so much to Karl Marx that he wanted to dedicate *Das Kapital* to Charles Darwin. Darwin refused. Mussolini invoked social Darwinism to justify his invasion of Abyssinia. Hitler used it to justify a program for the elimination of inmates of mental hospitals.

Because it is 'natural' it is therefore right is no basis for ethics. T. H. Huxley should be recognised as having given the knockout blow to the doctrine of social Darwinism in his Romanes Lecture of 1893. He argued that human cultural progress reverses the biological Darwinism of survival of the fittest. Social evolution is not to be achieved by a struggle for existence in which the weak go to the wall. The law of the jungle is not the law of civilisation.

A REALISTIC VIEW OF NATURE AND OUR HUMAN ROLE IN IT

Fortunately, besides the fables associated with a romantic view of nature there is a factually based practical view of nature and our role in it. This is the concept of the ecologically sustainable society. Despite successions of ice ages, floods, storms and earthquakes, nature persists, though in a changed state. The greatest changes in the past 10,000 years have almost certainly been brought through human activity. The differences in vegetation and fauna of Mediterranean countries over that period are mainly due to human activity. Forests were cut down both for timber and agriculture. In the Middle East and in Northern Africa the overexploitation of natural resources led to an increase in deserts which is still going on.

In some case the overexploitation of nature resulted in the demise of civilisations. This is almost certainly what happened with the Maya civilisation in Mexico. Forestry and agriculture became non-sustainable. Easter Island was one of the last places on Earth to be settled by human beings. First reached by Polynesians about 500 CE, this small island supported a sophisticated agricultural society by the sixteenth century. Easter Island has a semi-arid climate ameliorated by a verdant forest that trapped and held water. Its 7000 people raised crops and chickens and caught fish. They constructed a thousand massive eight metre high obsidian statues that were hauled across the island using tree trunks as rollers. By the time European settlers reached the island in the seventeenth century, these stone statues were the only remnants of a once impressive civilisation, one that had collapsed in a few decades. As the human population expanded more land was cleared for crops and the remaining trees were cut down for fuel. The lack of wood made it impossible to build fishing boats and houses, forcing people to live in caves. The loss of forests led to soil erosion, further diminishing food supplies. Armed conflict broke out. Some even resorted to cannibalism to survive. Easter Island presents a stark picture of what can happen when a human economy expands in the face of limited resources (Brown 1999 p. 11). The key limits for the world in the twenty-first century are freshwater, forests, rangelands, oceanic fisheries, biological diversity and the global atmosphere. The critical question is: will we recognise the world's natural limits or will we proceed to expand our ecological footprint until it is too late to turn back? We could well heed the Buddhist saying: 'Cut down the forest of your greed before cutting real trees.'

The lesson we have to learn is that human intervention can be very destructive and if we are to have a future our activities need to be managed in such as way that forestry and agriculture and all other uses of land are self-sustaining. There also has to be a limit to the area of the Earth that is used for these purposes if we are to curb the present extinction of species. It is just over a century since the first national parks in the world were established. These were Yellowstone in the USA and the Royal National Park just south of Sydney. Still only about 4.5 per cent of the Earth's land surface is protected in this way.

Our objective should be an ecologically sustainable society. The word society in this context refers to the society of plants, microorganisms and animals including humans. The idea of the ecologically sustainable society was the outcome of a discussion of limits to growth in the 1970s. The phrase limits to growth referred to the fact that resources needed by humans were limited on the face of the Earth and this imposes a limit on the number of people who can securely populate the Earth. That number depends upon the economic level of the inhabitants which can be measured by their 'standard of living', which is the amount of resources available per person and is usually measured by the GNP per capita. The discussion of limits to growth and the necessity of an ecologically sustainable society has led to moving the emphasis away from standard of living to quality of life.

This depends upon the recognition that life is more than food and raiment (standard of living) and involves the sorts of human needs discussed in chapter 2. There we recognised that quality of life goes up for poor people as their standard of living increases, but that beyond a certain level of standard of living the quality of life goes down. This latter trend is happening in rich countries today. So it becomes necessary when we are interested in quality of life of humans that we take account of what we are doing to the Earth and all its inhabitants. It is for this reason that the Worldwatch Institute in Washington was established in 1975. Each year this institute produces its *State of the World Report: Progress Toward a Sustainable Society*. The subtitle of the report indicates that it reports on the extent to which we are or are not moving toward an ecologically sustainable society. Here follow some assessments from the 1998 *State of the World Report* (Brown 1998) that indicate that all is not well with the Earth.

Fisheries are important resources for humans. There is what is called a sustainable yield threshold of a natural system such as an oceanic fishery. When that threshold of numbers fished is crossed (overfishing) the resource base itself (the capital) begins to be consumed. When the amount of fish caught surpasses the sustainable yield the fish stock begins to shrink. If fishing continues the fishery collapses and may never recover. The UN Food and Agriculture Organisation, which monitors oceanic fisheries, reports that nearly all fisheries are being overfished beyond the capacity for replacement.

The same is true of many forested regions of the Earth which are being cut for timber and for farms. Once the demand for forest products exceeds the sustainable yield of the forest it begins to shrink. As excess demand over sustainable yield widens, deforestation occurs. Within scarcely a generation countries such as Mauritania, Ethiopia and Haiti have been almost entirely deforested.

A similar principle applies to the use of water. If the growing demand for water exceeds the sustainable yield of an aquifer, the water table falls. When the aquifer is depleted the rate of pumping falls to the rate of recharge. If it falls below this, further cutbacks are necessary. Water tables are falling on every continent. Water use has tripled since mid-century, which has led to massive over-pumping. This has led to curtailment of irrigation. In many countries water diversion from rivers has reached the point where some rivers no longer make it to the sea. The Colorado, the major river in south-western United States, rarely reaches the Gulf of Mexico where it used to enter the sea.

Rangelands on all continents are being overgrazed with resultant soil erosion. They are less and less sustainable. Over half of all range-lands in Australia have such serious soil erosion that they no longer support the herds of sheep and cattle they once did. The world con-sumption of grain has tripled since mid-century. As a result, farmers have extended agriculture into marginal lands where continuous cropping is unsustainable. Soil erosion in agricultural lands in Africa has reduced Africa's total grain harvest by 8 per cent. The reduction is likely to be double that amount in the next decade if steps are not taken to reverse the trend.

Biodiversity is a buzzword these days. It refers to the number of species in any stated habitat. 'Keep them alive with you,' was the injunction Noah received when he was told to build the great ark. But have we done so? The extinction and decline in numbers of species all over the world has become horrific. This is mainly due to the destruction of habitats, especially forests. The United Nations Convention on Biological Diversity gave authority and motivation for maintaining ecological habitats. But what is achieved depends upon national governments. Australia is the only developed country which has a high level of species diversity. It is one of twelve mega-diverse countries. Ninety-two per cent of Australian indigenous mammals, 70 per cent of the land birds, 85 per cent of the flowering plants, 89 per cent of the reptiles and 93 per cent of the frogs are unique to Australia. They are not indigenous to any other country. But on the other side of the picture Australia has one of the worst records for extinction of species. Since 1788 about 90 per cent of the native vegetation in the eastern temperate zone has been removed, over 50 per cent of the rainforests have been cleared and the propor-tion of the continent covered by forest or woodland has been reduced by more than a third. As a consequence twenty species of mammals, ten species of birds and eighty-three species of plants are known to have become extinct. Australia now has a program to iden-tify the remaining habitats that need to be protected and to identify species under threat. It also has a program of land-care to reverse the extensive practice of unsustainable agriculture that destroys the resources of soil and water on which agriculture depends. It has been no easy task to try to reverse the destructive trends in the history of Australia, despite it being an economically well-off nation. How much more difficult is this for countries that are economically poor (Birch 1993b; Langmore 1995).

A wide range of indicators show that, globally, we are moving away from sustainability, not towards it (Eckersley 1998a). The 1998 report of the World Wide Fund for Nature includes a 'living planet index' based on an assessment of forest, freshwater and marine habitats. The index declined by 30 per cent between 1970 and 1995, 'meaning that the world has lost nearly a third of its natural wealth in that time'. In addition the WWFN estimate that, at the present rate, consumption of resources and pollution will double every fifteen years (WWFN 1998).

The ecologically sustainable society is not to be confused with 'sustainable development', which is a euphemism for continued economic growth. You cannot grow into sustainability. The recognition of the need for ecologically sustainable practices is one of the most striking examples of a clear-cut practical concept. It has had a global appeal, both because the phrase itself has an appeal that caught on and because it led to clear-cut change in practices that are realistic, such as land-care programs in various countries. We don't need to romance ecology to make it work.

Everything in this chapter to this point has emphasised the instrumental value of nature and its importance in conservation. But there is a second value to nature, and that is the intrinsic value of the creatures in it. I have discussed the meaning of intrinsic value in chapter 2, mainly in relation to human beings. Elsewhere I have discussed its meaning for non-humans (Birch 1993a; Birch & Vischer 1987). The gist of the argument is that individual entities such as chimpanzees, birds, frogs and living cells all have intrinsic value in themselves and for themselves quite independently of their instrumental value to us or to other creatures. What gives intrinsic value is feeling. Whatever feels has intrinsic value. And whatever feels has rights. There is a gradation of intrinsic value across the whole range of creatures depending upon the richness of experience of their lives. Correspondingly there is a gradation of rights. A chimpanzee has presumably a richer experience than a mosquito and therefore has greater rights. A total view of an environmental ethic would take account of the intrinsic value of creatures as well as their instrumental value. Conservationists have been faithful to this sort of ethic in their arguments for the conservation of whales and of primates such as gorillas and chimpanzees. But it is an ethic which should be extended to all nature.

The next chapter deals with our place in nature in an evolutionary perspective, embracing the whole of life from its beginning to its evolutionary climax.

6

PROCESSING TOWARDS LIFE

More and more, physicists dare to say that all nature is in some sense
life-like, that there is no absolutely new principle of life that
comes in at some point in cosmic evolution.

Charles Hartshorne (1984 p. 62)

Bertrand Russell said that either life is matter-like or matter is life-like. A proposition of process thought is that matter is life-like. The proposition that life is matter-like leads to the traditional reductionist analysis of living organisms that goes on in biological laboratories. The ultimate apotheosis of this approach is molecular biology. Reductionist analyses are analyses of the objective aspects of living organisms such as the conduction of electrical impulses in nerves or the biochemistry of the formation of blood. As a methodology reductionism is appropriate, provided due recognition is given to its limitations.

In contemporary biology, subjective aspects of life such as consciousness, purpose and free will are either ignored or else attempts are made to reduce the subjective to the objective. Instead we take another approach as described in chapter 3. There are two points of view—inside and outside, subjective and objective. In process thought the subjective, which we known in our own experience, applies all down the line from people to protons. Processing towards life is a metaphor for cosmic evolution from a relatively undifferentiated universe right after the big bang, for example a universe consisting of hydrogen atoms only. Whitehead's two lectures entitled 'Nature and Life', delivered at the University of Chicago, were essentially saying that an understanding of cosmic evolution had to be informed by a concept of what life is. The concept of what life is proposes that the individual entities of existence, or 'the really real things which in their collective unity compose the evolving universe' are 'occasions of experience' (Whitehead 1938 p. 151). That is an amazing thought, to put experience right at the foundations of the universe. In a universe that consisted of hydrogen atoms alone, the sum total of occasions of experience then must have been virtually minimal in cosmic history. The internal relations of that universe must have been tiny compared with a universe that has in it plants and animals including us. What has happened in between a universe that consisted of hydrogen alone and the universe that that includes us?

One aspect of the story is told by scientists in their account of cosmic and biological evolution. This is an account of the evolution of (what they see as) objects. Individual organisms are investigated as if they were machines, devoid of self-determination or spontaneity in any sense and so subject only to external forces. They are objects, not subjects. The alternative view of this book is that the ultimate entities of the universe are subjects with their own degree of spontaneity, self-determination, freedom and sensateness or experience. This is the doctrine of panexperientalism. Griffin (1998 pp. 89–92) gives nine reasons for seriously considering this approach to reality. It is not my purpose to pursue all these reasons here. Instead I ask: are there any leads from the world of science of today suggesting that the individual entities of creation from protons to people are not simply objects pushed around by external forces? There is one, I suggest, that arises from what is called complexity theory. It proposes that sufficiently large systems of parts with enough interactions will generate totally new, but simple, laws of *self-organisation* that help to explain what has happened in evolution.

SELF-ORGANISATION IN COSMIC AND BIOLOGICAL EVOLUTION

Physicists and cosmologists regard self-organisation as the source of order in cosmic evolution up to and including the origin of life. Some of them, notably Paul Davies, have said that the onus is now on biologists to demonstrate the importance of self-organisation in biological evolution.

An example from physics of what is meant by self-organisation is the formation of the myriad symmetrical shapes of snowflakes. Probably no two snowflakes are alike. Snowflakes are formed by crystals of ice that generally have a hexagonal pattern. Often the pattern is beautifully intricate. The size and shape of a snowflake depends mainly on temperature and the amount of water vapour available as they form. The details of the design are dependent upon the environment in which the snowflake forms. In all this, physical forces are involved, pushing atoms of water this way and that. Many simple physical systems exhibit spontaneous order of this sort. An oil droplet in water forms a sphere. Lipids in water form hollow bilipid membrane spheres, such as cell membranes. Further examples of self-organisation in physics are given by Paul Davies (1989 pp. 72–92).

Consider now some examples of self-organisation in biology at different levels of organisation. It seems likely that the self-repeating patterns generated by growth processes of plants that result in the spiral symmetry (spiral phyllotaxis) of a sunflower or a pine cone are best understood in terms of self-organisation. The spiral rows of scales in a pine cone and the arrangement of seeds in a sunflower conform, in their mathematical arrangement, to the famous Fibonacci series of numbers. The apical growing point gives rise to spirals turning clockwise and spirals turning anti-clockwise, with the numbers of the two sets being adjacent integers of the Fibonacci series 3:5, 5:8, 8:13 (Kauffman 1995 p. 151; Stewart 1998 pp. 123–4).

A simple virus, such as the tobacco mosaic virus, forms by self-assembly in which all the participating proteins are organised into a complexly structured viral coat. If the parts of these viruses are disassembled they spontaneously reassemble. More complex viruses cannot do this (Wood 1987). Another example of self-organisation at the molecular level is the local interaction among amino acids which give rise to complexly folded protein molecules. When the complex protein molecule is dissociated from a three-dimensional state to a simpler linear state it is followed by spontaneous reassembly. They are not always able to so self-organise without guidance from the charmingly named chaperone proteins which guide the three-dimensional folding of proteins.

Spontaneous self-organisation is invoked by biochemists in the evolution of the prebiotic world in which a variety of atoms assembled into organic molecules, eventually giving rise to molecules of RNA, DNA and proteins which led to further complex assemblies and eventually to cells. Manfred Eigen coined the term 'molecular self-organisation' to describe molecular evolution that could have given rise to the origin of life. A summary of some of these processes is given by Fritjof Capra (1996 p. 75–150) and Paul Davies (1998). Kauffman sees the origin of life, not as an incalculably improbable accident but as 'an expected fulfilment of the natural order' as a result of the phenomenon of self-organisation (Kauffman 1995 p. 20). Most of Kauffman's long book deals with mathematical models and some biochemical models of 'non equilibrium ordered systems' that lead to spontaneous self-organisation into more complex structures. The universe soon after the big bang consisted of only one sort of entity—hydrogen atoms. In this epoch the universe was astonishingly featureless. Today the living world consists of at least 10 million different small organic molecules and at least one trillion different proteins. Where did all this diversity come from? Kauffman's book is devoted to answering this question in terms of the principle of self-organisation.

Until recently self-organisation had been little recognised in living organisms. All the examples which follow were, until recently, interpreted in terms of centralised organisation. However, recent studies provide evidence that in each of the following examples the order is a consequence of self-organisation and not centralised organisation. The evidence is given in each case.

Notable examples are the slime moulds that live in soil. Spores of slime moulds on germination produce amoeba-like cells. These cells immediately disperse as though mutually repelled from each other. Provided they have sufficient bacteria, which is their food in the soil, they divide like amoebae by simple fission. When food becomes scarce the amoeba-like cells tend to distribute themselves uniformly and no longer repel one another. Then they aggregate at a number of centres to form at each centre a slug-like creature that slithers over the surface of the soil. It may reach a diameter of twenty-five centimetres or more. From this apparently undifferentiated mass of cells a stalk grows at the top of which a fruiting body is formed that develops spores. The fruiting body bursts to distribute its spores and so the strange life-cycle continues. What causes these changes? The present understanding is that a chemical substance called acrasin is secreted by the amoebae when they run out of food. The amoebae move up a gradient of acrasin, resulting in their aggregation to form the slug. Many different species of slime mould may live in the same place. How is it then that the cells of the different species don't get mixed up in aggregation? The answer is that different species secrete different acrasins. There is some evidence also that concentration waves of a chemical substance governs the production of the stalk and fruiting body. The effect of the concentration wave is to activate genes whose message is: produce a fruiting body (Bonner, 1982; Hagan & Cohen 1981).

Resnick simulated the aggregation of slime mould cells in a computer model (Resnick 1995 pp. 232–3) Each 'creature' in his model is given the characteristic corresponding to the emission of a chemical substance while also following the gradient of this chemical substance.

The chemical is given a finite life corresponding to its rate of evaporation. With this decentralised strategy the 'creatures' aggregate into clusters on his computer screen.

With such examples in mind we can define self-organisation as 'patterns determined, not by some centralised authority, but by local interactions about decentralised components' (Resnick 1995 p. 229). It is a process of ordering from a less ordered state to a more ordered state. Self-organisation is contrasted with centralised organisation, such for example as the production of order by DNA in the cell. This has led to the classical model that evolution is change in the organising molecules of DNA and RNA. So we can recognise two forms of organisation in living organisms, self-organisation and centralised organisation.

Craig Reynolds investigated the flocking of birds using computer models. He dubbed his creatures 'boids'. His boids were given three rules: try to match direction with your neighbours, head for their average position, and don't collide. Nowhere do the rules tell the boids to move in flocks, yet the boids do just that. It seems that flocks just happen. The flock can change direction. This could happen as a result of one bird suddenly making a mistake and changing direction. Its neighbours try to share the error as they try to follow the average direction of boids around them. The error begins to spread through the whole flock. The point of the story is that each boid follows the rules of the game and the result is a flock without their being any central organising control of their aggregate behaviour (Ammons 1999).

Another example of self-organisation in biology is the construction of a termite nest with its complex chambers. Termites construct their complex nests in an orderly fashion that, at least in part, is guided by chemical gradients. Termites are among the master architects of the animal world. When a termite deposits a lump of earth on the base of the forthcoming nest it deposits at the same time a chemical that attracts other termites to the same place to deposit their lumps of earth there and so form a pillar. That is but one aspect of the building of a complexly structured nest by a large number of individual termites cooperating together. Each termite colony has a queen (Prigogine & Stengers 1984 p. 186). But, as in ant colonies, the queen does not 'tell' the termites what to do. The queen is more like a mother than a ruling queen. There is no-one in charge of a master plan. Rather, each termite carries out a relatively simple task. Termites are practically blind, so they must interact with each other and the world around them primarily through the senses of touch and smell. From local interactions among thousands of termites impressive structures emerge.

Resnick has made computer models of some of the steps in the construction of a termite nest (Resnick 1995). As he points out, the construction of an entire termite nest would be a monumental project. Instead he proceeded with a simple model to program termites to collect wood chips and put them in piles. At the start of the program wood chips were scattered randomly throughout the termites' world. The challenge was to make the termites organise chips into a few orderly piles. He made each individual termite obey the following two rules:

1 If you are not carrying anything and you bump into a wood chip, pick it up.
2 if you are carrying a wood chip and you bump into another wood chip, put down the wood chip you are carrying.

The program worked. At first the termites gathered the wood chips into hundreds of small piles, but gradually the number of piles declined while the number of wood chips in surviving piles increased.

AntFarm is a computer program that simulates the foraging strategies of ants (Coveney & Highfield 1995). Many ants obeying simple rules produce their complex foraging behaviour. Self-organising ants require just four rules to be followed:

1 If an ant finds food, take it to the nest and mark the trail with a chemical substance called a pheromone.
2 If an ant crosses the trail and has no food, follow the trail to food.
3 If an ant returns to the nest, deposit the food and wander back along the trail.
4 If the above three rules do not apply, wander at random.

Another striking example of self-organisation in animal behaviour is the swarm-raid of the army ant (Franks 1989 pp. 139–45). A raid consists of a dense phalanx of up to 200,000 workers that march relentlessly across the forest floor. The column of raiders can be up to twenty metres wide. The raiders leave in their wake, not only a trail of carnage, but also a series of connected columns along which the victorious army ant workers run with their booty. These columns all lead to the principal trail of the raid, which links the swarm front to the temporary bivouac. It is inconceivable that a tiny individual within the 200 metre long raid has any knowledge of the plan of the raid as a whole. The structure of the swarm can be achieved by simple, self-organising interactions among the raiding ants. Franks (1989) devised computer simulations in which moving ants lay down chemical trails which organise the movement patterns of other individuals throughout the developing raid. His simulations mimic, with some precision, real raids. His models show how the collective behaviour of the swarm can be achieved with no central coordination, but instead through the communication between foragers by the laying down of, and reaction to, trail chemicals.

In each of these models of social insects the emphasis is that the order of the colony is a consequence of the activity of individual members of the colony. There may well be another element involved in the life of these social insects and that is the idea that individual behaviour is also a result of their reaction to each other. This aspect has been emphasised by Goodwin (1998). He cites the case of a rhythmic activity of young workers of the ant *Leptothorax* tending the queen and the young in brood chambers. The team of workers are active for a time and then become inactive, taking about half an hour to go through one cycle. It appears that when the density of ants reaches a certain level the group of ants begin to display this cyclic activity. What happens is that an active ant that contacts an inactive ant by means of its antennae causes the inactive ant to become active. This results eventually in group activity. This component of ant activity can readily be simulated in a computer program. The programmed 'ants' become active as a group. There is nothing mysterious about this. The model is simply recognising that a component of the environment of any ant are other ants. This is hardly surprising.

In colonies of social insects, workers perform a variety of tasks such as foraging, brood care and nest construction. As the needs of the colony change and as resources become available, colonies adjust the numbers of workers engaged in each task. Task allocation is the process that results in specific workers being engaged in specific tasks in numbers appropriate to the current situation. Until the mid 1980s research emphasised the internal factors within an individual that determine its task. Internal factors had to do with body size, age and genetic constitution. However, in recent years it has become evident that division of labour had more to do with environment and that it is rare for individuals to specialise in particular tasks throughout their lives. From day to day or even hour to hour an individual worker may perform a variety of tasks, changing its task as circumstances require. For example, a honey bee forager's decision whether to collect nectar or remain in the nest depends on how much nectar is already stored in the nest. As a result of investigating these phenomena, Deborah Gordon (1996) makes the following assessment of what is happening:

> Task allocation operates without any central or hierarchical control to direct individuals into particular tasks. The queen does not issue commands, and workers do not direct the behaviour of other workers. We can compare the diverse tasks performed by a colony to the many proteins generated by gene transcription, to various cell types of a developing embryo, or to the firing patterns of neurones in the brain. What all these have in common is that, without any central control, individual units (genes, cells, neurones or workers) respond to simple, local information, in ways that allow the whole system (cells, brains, organisms or colonies) to function: the appropriate number of units performs each activity at the appropriate time. (p. 121)

There is, in the above quotation, the important suggestion that self-organisation may help to elucidate one of the most complex ordering processes in living organisms, as yet little understood, namely development from egg to adult. We do know that a thousand million bits of information stored in the genes contain the digital instructions for making an organism. These are present in the single cell of the egg. The initial single cell of the egg of any animal undergoes a number of cell divisions to produce a mass of similar cells. At some subsequent stage differentiation of these cells proceeds as they multiply further. Some become muscle cells, others nerve cells and so on. All coordinate to become a unitary organism of millions of cells with a body plan that is different for different organisms. Muscle cells are different from nerve cells, not because they have different genes, their genes are the same. However, different genes are switched on in different environments. How the appropriate genes are switched on in appropriate places remains a problem. One proposal involves chemical gradients. For example, in the fruit fly the first difference between the front and back end of the egg is caused by the cells of the mother's ovary, external to the egg, that release at the anterior end a specific chemical which then diffuses backwards, giving rise to a chemical gradient of concentration. This in turn could cause different genes to be switched on in different places. A single gradient cannot set up a whole pattern, but a succession of such processes might. We know that chemical gradients are involved in the ordering of the building of a termite nest and in the life history of slime moulds. It is possible that in embryonic development similar sorts of ordering are at least initiated by chemical gradients (Maynard Smith 1995). In his little book, *Shaping Life*, Maynard Smith (1998) gives a very clear account of what we know and what we do not know about the processes that go on in embryonic development. He considers that during the past ten years there has been a revolution in our understanding of these complex processes that is little appreciated outside biology. It has involved a bringing together of development and evolution.

Self-organisation is part of the research program of so-called complexity theory at the Santa Fe Institute for the Study of Complex Systems. The approach of the research workers in this institute is highly theoretical. As Lewontin has remarked, complexity theory 'proposes that sufficiently large systems of parts with enough inter-action will generate totally new, but simple "laws of organisation" that will explain, among other things, us' (Lewontin 1996 p. 26). The behaviour of these models turns out to be what are, in the math-ematical sense, chaotic. Kauffman (1993) argues that chaotic systems can give rise to structures 'for free', instead of each detail of structure having been forged independently by natural selection. According to this interpretation of his models, the system leaps spontaneously into a state of greater organised complexity. This is what Kauffman calls self-organisation. The devotees of this approach have been criticised by geneticists and evolutionists as practising 'fact-free' science in con-trast to ordinary 'earth-bound' genetics (Dover 1996; Maynard Smith 1995). It is a question for the future as to whether or not Kauffman's models will be heuristically valuable for biology.

These models may even be applicable to complex problems in human societies. In the 1990s war in Yugoslavia the country blew itself apart. This was a society that was technically advanced with uni-versities, libraries and all the advice in the world from the interna-tional community. Yet it blew itself to pieces. Possibly a quarter of a million men, women and children died in the process. And how they died, from all sorts of atrocities. More than 2 million people were dri-ven out of their homes, many were deprived of everything but what they could carry in their arms. With one or two exceptions the sur-viving separated states are impoverished, degraded and corrupted. Much of the problem may be due to tyranny from the top. But much of it also may be a consequence of what individual people feel towards others of different origin, religion and history. The self-organisation modeller could ask: why not try a predictive model, not at the macro level, but one that focuses on local interactions and change at that level? The pressure toward war, peace or anarchy that is driven from within is very difficult to control from without. This concept was at the heart of much that Plato had to say about the ills of society. It was his unerring insight into human nature that traced the source of public tyranny in the state to the tyranny of lawless pas-sion within the individual. Could this anarchy be modelled on a com-puter? This is a question for future nerds.

All the examples I have given of self-organisation in biology are explained by biologists in strictly mechanistic terms, complex though these mechanisms usually are. Some of the processes can be replicated to some extend on a computer. But this does not necessarily imply that the behaving entities are in all respects machines. Paul Davies (1998) concludes his book on the origin of life with the following statement about an alternative view to sheer mechanism and a universe of chance and chance alone:

> It is the vision of a self-organising and self-complexifying universe, governed by ingenious laws that encourage matter to evolve towards life and consciousness. [It is] a universe in which the emergence of thinking beings is a fundamental and integral part of the overall scheme of things. (p. 227)

The importance of this statement is the notion of a tendency towards life and mind. Earlier in this final chapter Davies quotes a number of biochemists who speak of matter having an 'innate tendency to grope in the direction of life' (p. 209) by virtue of the chemical affinities that act between atoms and molecules and of 'inherent properties of atoms and molecules', which seem to direct organisation towards life. On page 227 Davies writes:

> Only if there is more to it [the origin of life and its evolution] than chance, only if nature has an ingeniously built-in bias towards life and mind, would we expect to see anything like the developmental thrust that has occurred on Earth [to be] repeated on other planets.

Davies is saying that we could hardly expect life to exist elsewhere in the universe if the processes involved were matters of chance and law alone. Something else comes into the picture. Perhaps in his wisdom, he leaves this as an open speculation for others to follow up. Others have to some extent done this, though not necessarily in a way with which Davies' would concur. This is the subject of the sections which follow.

SELF-ORGANISATION AND INTERNAL RELATIONS

Self-organisation is exactly what we might expect of Whitehead's individual entities. Each individual entity, be it a proton, a protein molecule, an amoeba of a slime mould or an ant in an army raid, can be regarded as being what it is largely by virtue of its internal relations to its environment, be those components of environment temperature for a snowflake, acrasin for an amoeba or a neighbour ant for another ant. Each entity is then seen as a subject relating internally to its environment. An internal relation is one that alters the nature, even the very being, of the entity concerned. Each is having experiences, unconscious though they may be. Individual entities conform to Charles Kingsley's proposition in his novel *The Water Babies* that God makes things that make themselves. They have self-creativity.

Whitehead enunciated more clearly than anyone how creative evolution of living organisms cannot be understood if the elements composing them are conceived as individual entities that maintain exactly their identity throughout all the changes and interactions, as is the case with the parts of a machine or in the Newtonian model of the universe. Complex living organisms can be broken down into their component parts such as their cells. How is it that the whole has properties the components do not have? It is evident that the properties of the whole are not found in the parts, except as they are organised in the whole. Hence the statement of Lewontin, Rose and Kamin (1984): 'as one moves up a level the properties of each larger whole are given not merely by the units of which it is composed but of the organising relations between them ... these organising relationships mean that the properties of matter relevant at one level are just inapplicable at other levels' (p. 278).

In this perspective, cosmic and biological evolution are not simply the evolution of objects that are reorganised by change in their external relations (e.g., natural selection) but *change in internal relations of subjects*. It is the evolution of subjects. A subject is an individual entity that has a degree of self-determination. It has some degree of mentality that is presumably minuscule in the proton compared the person. Of course we don't know what it is like to be a proton or an electron and to have its subjective experience of being what it is. There is a distinction between knowing something from within and knowing something from without. The only individual entity that we know from within is ourselves. We can only infer the within of other individual entities. The important point is the proposition that mentality is not just in a corner of nature. It is pervasive. Subjectivity is part and parcel of the warp and woof of creation in space and time. After all, our subjective experience is the only thing each of us is really sure of. The rest is speculation.

Process thought sees human experience as a high level exemplification of reality in general. David Griffin (1998) argues that the idea that nature's ultimate units are 'vacuous actualities' without any subjectivity is even more speculative than the concept of nature's ultimate units as experiential. We know from our own experience that experiencing actualities can exist. But we have no experiential knowledge that a vacuous actuality is even possible. The only reality we known first hand from the inside is our own. Yet it would be odd to scoff at the notion that all reality has the same basic architecture of inside and outside, agent and patient, ends and means. 'Of course,' says Hartshorne (1997), 'a rock does not feel, and neither I think does a tree. But the ever-active atoms or molecules of the one or cells of the other may do so. What could tell us that they do not? To this question I have for long been awaiting an answer' (p.12). In this quotation Hartshorne uses the word 'feel' in Whitehead's sense of being internally related or having some degree of subjectivity. He is not referring to conscious experience. The word 'experience' in this way of thinking includes non-conscious experience. This is not a contradiction in terms. We talk about the subconscious as a realm below the level of consciousness. Much of therapeutic psychiatry has been concerned with bringing the subconscious to the conscious level. There is the 'tip of the tongue' effect when we can't remember something but it comes to consciousness after a few moments thinking about it.

LIVING AND NON-LIVING SOCIETIES

But you may ask: at what point does life appear in the processing? The answer is: at no point. For matter is life-like. However, it is convenient to make some distinctions. An electron or an atom or a molecule is each considered to have some iota of freedom and self-determination. But it is minimal at this level. It is not meaningful to call them alive. The difference between a molecule and a cell is sufficiently great to call the cell alive. The difference is in the degree of novelty, for life is tied up with novelty. What is novel is the capacity for experience. For the most part a molecule of water is a molecule of water and that's that. Not so with us. Each of us starts off our lives as a single cell. Then we become a bunch of cells, all rather similar. Eventually these cells give rise to daughter cells that differentiate. Some become muscle cells, others nerve cells, others skin cells and so on. Each lives a different sort of life. In process terms we would say each cell has a different sort of experience. Each has a novel experience. By contrast, the molecule of water retains its self-identity and its lowly self-determination and its iota of experience. A living society such as a cell or a human being experiences in its being a novel element which is not derived from the past. That is what novel means.

Whitehead (1929a) says 'the primary meaning of "life" is the origination of conceptual novelty—novelty of appetition' (p. 102). His point is that life has an anticipatory aspect about it which gives it novelty. The more alive the more novelty. The novelty in the atom or molecule is minimal. Not so in the cell. There is no definite proof of such an hypothesis. The only proof is elucidation. If this way of looking at things enables us to see in a new light aspects of the world formerly shrouded in darkness of incomprehension, then it has gained some measure of confirmation.

Novelty is not mere change. The ever-present entropic tendency to decay is change. That tendency can be resisted in two ways. One way is by the very stable structure of many things such as rocks. These endure by countless repetition of unchanging patterns. The second way it can be overcome locally is by creative novelty which rises above external determination. That is to be alive. Hence life is directed against the repetitious mechanisms of the universe. There is an urge in life to meet life's as yet unrealised possibilities. 'The universe is creative advance into novelty,' says Whitehead (1929a p. 222).

We are now in a position to make some distinctions. Electrons, atoms and molecules are example of individual entities. Each has an organic unity and in process thought each is considered to act and feel (experience) as one. That is the definition of an *individual entity*.

A rock is different. It has a structure and relationship between the molecules that constitute it. So in a sense it is society of molecules. But it does not act and feel as one. It has no organic unity. It is a *non-living society*. The same can be said of a crystal, a star or a sun. A pile of rocks is different again. There is no structural relationship between the rocks in a pile except that one rests on another. The pile of rocks can be called an *aggregate*.

PROGRESS IN EVOLUTION?

A fundamental question to ask about cosmic evolution is why the universe that at one time consisted of hydrogen atoms and nothing else didn't just stay that way? Why did it go on to evolve other sorts of atoms, complex molecules, cells and countless species of plants and animals, including us? Whitehead's proposition is that on the one hand the individual entities themselves at any stage have a propensity for creativity and that this urge is met by the potentiality of the universe from its foundations for all sorts of possibilities to be realised. The creative urge of the creature is met by cosmic lure. A musical note on a tuning fork elicits a response from a piano because the piano already has in it a string tuned to that same note. So it is with us. So it is with the rest of the individual entities of creation.

This perspective appears to be counter to an emphasis by some biologists, notably that of Gould (1996), in interpreting biological evolution. 'Natural evolution,' says Gould, 'includes no principle of predictable progress or movement to greater complexity' (p. 222).

The picture of evolution is not that of an escalator ever going upwards but of a branching radiating bush. Living organisms diverge from one another to meet particular needs in their various environments. Our own species is one among many in the ever-branching tree of life.

Since complexity of organisation has frequently been used as a measure of progress in evolution, Gould equates the word progress with complexity. There is no inevitability, says Gould, that there will be an increase in complexity with time. Bacteria must have been amongst the earliest organisms to evolve some billions of years ago. And they haven't changed much. They do what they do pretty well and there are more of them, both in kind and numbers, than of any other sort of organism. There is no law that says they have to change. 'The Age of Bacteria', argues Gould, was an age that persisted for billions of years from near the beginning right up to now. Bacteria alone formed the tree of life for the first 2 billion years, about half of life's full history. We still live in the Age of Bacteria. Bacteria are a classic example of persistence with little change. Other organisms have changed from a complex state to a less complex one. Many intestinal parasites have lost most of their organs to become simple sacs with few organs to deal with reproduction and the digested nutrients they absorb from the intestine of their host. They have lost rather than gained complexity.

There are sequences of evolution which Gould recognises as progressive trends in complexity, such as the increase in size of the brain of *Homo* over the last 2 million years. But there is no law that says the brain must go on increasing in size. It has got to a point where it seems to be doing a pretty good job in enabling humans to survive, provided we don't decide to destroy ourselves. Trends of this sort are not a consequence of some inner urge to become more complex. They are the natural outcome of a particular sort of organisation which is adaptive, that continues so long as it has adaptive value for the organism. Its continuance is a consequence of natural selection.

The history of biological evolution is also the history of dead ends such as the dinosaurs. The tree of life is not like a single ladder with bacteria on the bottom rung and humans on the top with increasing complexity in between. It is more like a tree with myriads of branches, many of them dead ones. Indeed it is the fate of all species to become extinct.

While simple forms dominate in most environments, Gould (1996) concedes that there is an increase in complexity of the most complex organisms and that human beings are probably more complex than anything that preceded them. But he adds: 'I fervently deny that this limited fact can provide an argument for general progress as a defining thrust of life's history' (p. 169). His reason for saying this is that if you look at organisms, not just at the beginning, when life had its minimal complexity, but at any subsequent time in evolutionary history, there is no evidence that these organisms in the course of time led to more complex creatures. Some did, but sometimes the movement went in the opposite direction.

What seems to have happened in evolution is that every conceivable ecological niche gets occupied. If the occupants are simple bacteria and no-one else can do the job as well then there is no cause for them to be pushed out by more complex creatures. It might happen that a more complex organism might do the job better, in which case they would probably invade the niche. Or an even less complex organism may invade the niche. In this sense every step in the evolution of a new organism (be it an increase or decrease in complexity) is a creative advance into novelty.

Gould's argument has the merit that it warns us not to be too simplistic about identifying trends in evolution. Yet none of what he says is counter to the proposition that every creature has its inborn propensity to survive and reproduce. This can be measured in objective terms of survival and reproduction and biologists do just that. But the principle can be interpreted subjectively, as Whitehead does in terms of an urge to live. Human beings, for example, experience an urge toward novelty of experience and more satisfying experience. When it disappears the quality of human life and even life's physical manifestations cease to exist. The same subjective principle can be applied to other organisms, be they simple bacteria, dinosaurs or cats and dogs. Evolutionary biologists for the most part deal with living organisms as objects and not as subjects, so it is not altogether surprising that they do not take account of the subjective. To so take account is not to invoke some mystical force but to regard the subjective as real both in interpreting animal behaviour (as Donald R. Griffin does in his book, *Animal Minds*) and as I am suggesting in interpreting evolution. So Whitehead (1938) wrote:

> Science can find no aim in nature: Science can find no creativity in nature; it finds mere rules of succession. These negations are true of natural science. They are inherent in its methodology. The reason for this blindness of physical science lies in the fact that such science deals with half the evidence provided by human experience. It divides the seamless coat—or, to change the metaphor into a happier form, it examines the coat, which is superficial, and neglects the body which is fundamental. (p. 154)

THE PAST, THE PRESENT AND THE FUTURE

My understanding is that there are two elements in internal relations, be the actual entity a proton or a person or anything in between such as an army ant. One is that the entity has internal relations with its immediate past. A well-known example is what we call memory, which is also an example of non-sensory perception (Whitehead's prehension). The other is that the entity has the aim of constituting its present occasion both for immediate satisfaction and for the sake of the anticipated possible future state. 'Life,' says Whitehead (1938), 'is the enjoyment of emotion derived from the past and aimed at the future' (p. 167). Somewhere else he says that the present is the fringe memory tinged with anticipation. The past is a real cause, so too possibilities are real (final) causes. And so too are external or mechanical (efficient) causes.

The evolutionary history of life suggested to Whitehead that there is an ever-present urge which can be interpreted as purposive. It can be seen as an aim to greater richness of experience or higher levels of subjective satisfaction. This does not mean that every successive step in evolution involved an increase in richness of experience of the entity being evolved. It does mean that from the foundations of the universe there was the possibility (not the inevitability) of all sorts of experience, including self-conscious experience that we know in ourselves. For Whitehead (1929b p. 8) the art of life is first to be alive, secondly to be alive in a satisfactory way, and thirdly to acquire an increase in satisfaction. We know how this is true of human life. The conduct of human affairs is dominated by our recognition of foresight determining purpose and purpose issuing in conduct. Whitehead (1929b) comments that 'Scientists animated by the purpose of proving that they are purposeless constitute an interesting subject for study' (p. 16).

In writing about purpose Whitehead was discussing not just human life but life in general. The extreme rejection of final causation (purpose) from our categories of explanation has been fallacious. The 'vacuous actualities' of classical physics cannot evolve. They can only be rearranged as substances. 'On this theory,' says Whitehead (1929b), 'all that there is to be known is that inexplicable bits of matter are hurrying about with their motions correlated by inexplicable laws expressible in terms of their spatial relations to each other. If this be the final dogmatic truth, philosophy can have nothing to say to natural science' (p. 50). The process view is that each actual entity from protons to people is an occasion of experience which is the outcome of its own purpose. As Charles Hartshorne (1987) says: 'I believe that the most significant model we can have even of the simplest parts of the universe, say molecules, atoms, and particles, is that they are the simplest, most primitive cases of that which our own natures illustrate in vastly more complex and highly evolved forms' (p. 120).

In the process perspective biological evolution is seen, not just as involving mechanical changes say to the heart as a pump, but internal changes whereby the experience or internal relations become richer in a human being as compared with a mosquito. 'Creativity,' said Whitehead (1929a), 'is the principle of novelty' (p. 21). What then is creatively novel about evolutionary change? There is novelty along the route in the sense that human experience is novel and presumably richer compared to the experience of a dinosaur. A world of dinosaurs without humans is a different world from one that contains humans. But human experience has a continuity in origin from the feelings that constituted the being of the first mammals, the reptiles from which they evolved and all individual entities prior to them in the evolutionary sequence going back to the physicists' initially featureless universe. Something is achieved in the process. To call that something creative advance or novelty is less ambiguous and less misleading than the term progress.

There exists the counter tendency of entropy in which organisation becomes less with the passage of time and the universe as we know it will no longer exist. In the big crunch at the end of the universe all may again be compressed to a singularity, which is what the physicist calls that infinitely small and infinitely compressed state of affairs that gave rise to the big bang, which might start all over again.

What is the point of it all? There seem to me only two answers to that question. Cosmologist Steven Weinberg (1977) held that, without permanence, 'The more the universe seems comprehensible, the more it also seems pointless' (p. 149). That bleak view I reject. In similar vein physicist Richard Feynman (1998) wrote: 'the great accumulation of understanding as to how the physical world behaves only convinces one that this behavior has a kind of meaninglessness about it' (p. 32). There is a second answer to this question. There is a meaning to it all. That is the subject of the next chapter.

7

IS GOD NECESSARY?

One of the reasons for the late modern denial of any kind of
cosmic mind was that all such notions became suspect
by association with the supernaturalistic conception of such a mind.

David Griffin (1998 p. 209)

Chapter 6 concluded with a quotation from astrophysicist Steven Weinberg proclaiming that the more we know about the universe the more meaningless it becomes. By contrast, physicist Paul Davies (1992) concluded his book *The Mind of God* by saying that a universe that produces beings who are self-aware cannot be the 'minor byproduct of mindless, purposeless forces. We are truly meant to be here' (p. 232). Davies' view is developed further in his later book where he speaks of life as having 'emerged more or less on cue as part of the deep lawfulness of the cosmos—it is scripted into the great cosmic drama in a basic manner—it hints at a universe with a purpose' (Davies 1998 p. 3).

There could hardly be a greater contrast between the conclusions about the universe drawn by these two physicists, Weinberg and Davies. Both authors have written a great deal about cosmic history. Both of them subscribe to the big bang scenario of the origin of the universe. In the beginning was the singularity—the physicist's term for a point of infinite compression. If one imagines a film of 20 billion years of cosmic evolution running backwards, the nebulae and galaxies would get closer and closer to each other and eventually all the universe would be packed together in a point of infinite density in which the distance between anything would be zero. This is the singularity that exploded in the big bang when time is said to have begun. Some physicists push the universe back further, but that hardly concerns us here. First radiation dominated the universe. After a time matter instead of radiation was dominant. As the universe expanded and cooled the fundamental particles formed and got together as atoms. Forces of gravitation resulted in these coming together leading to stars, galaxies and planets. Some 10 to 20 billion years later we find the universe as it is today being studied and comprehended by our minds. That needs explanation.

THE UNNECESSARY GOD

In *The Brothers Karamazov* Dostoievski takes us to Seville in Spain in the most terrible time of the Inquisition when fires were lighted every day to burn heretics. And Jesus appeared. He came to the hot pavement of this southern town in which on the day before his arrival almost a hundred heretics had been burnt, *ad majorem Dei gloriam*, by the cardinal, the Grand Inquisitor. The people surround Jesus, flock about him and follow him. He moves among them with a gentle smile of infinite passion. He holds out his hands to the people and blesses them. Healing virtue comes from contact with him. He stops at the steps of the great cathedral. At that moment the cardinal passes by his cathedral. He sees all. He holds out his finger and bids the guards take Jesus. And in the midst of a death-like silence they lay hands on him and lead him away to the close, gloomy, vaulted prison in the ancient palace of the Inquisition and shut him in. In the pitch darkness the iron door of the prison is suddenly opened. The Grand Inquisitor himself comes in with a lamp in his hand. He stands in the doorway and for a minute gazes into Jesus' face. The Inquisitor speaks: 'Is it thou? Thou?' Receiving no answer, he adds at once: 'Don't answer, be silent. What canst thou say, indeed? I know too well what thou wouldst say. And thou hast no right to add anything to what thou hadst said of old. Why then art thou come to hinder us?' Jesus said not a word.

Suddenly Jesus approaches the Inquisitor and kisses him softly on his bloodless lips. That was his answer. The Inquisitor shudders. His lips move. He goes to the door, opens it and says to Jesus: 'Go and come no more' and leads him into the dark alleys of the town. The prisoner goes away.

The Grand Inquisitor has entered the churches of our time wearing the strong, tight-fitting armour of literalism, supernaturalism, exclusivity, narrow moralism, homophobia, sexism and fundamentalism. The God which the Grand Inquisitor protects is almighty invincible power, a king and magic-worker who demands obedience of his subjects. As Whitehead (1929a) wrote:

> When the Western world accepted Christianity, Caesar conquered ...
> The brief Galilean ministry of humility flickered throughout the ages,
> uncertainly ... The church gave unto God the attributes which belonged
> exclusively to Caesar ... There is, however, in the Galilean origins of
> Christianity another suggestion which does not emphasise the ruling
> Caesar, or the ruthless moralist, or the unmoved mover. It dwells upon
> the tender elements of the world, which slowly and in quietness oper-
> ate by love; and finds purpose in the present immediacy of a kingdom
> not of this world. (pp. 342–3)

Primo Levi, who lived through the experience of a concentration camp, concluded from his terrible experience: 'Auschwitz exists, therefore God does not exist'. How can one reconcile the horrors of a concentration camp with an almighty God? The answer is you can't. The more accurate statement would be: Auschwitz exists, therefore God is either not almighty or if he is almighty then God is malevolent. It is no wonder that the experience of horror in a concentration camp led many inmates to reject the God they were brought up to believe or else to change their conception of God. Australia had its Port Arthur massacre in which thirty-five innocent people were slaughtered by a crazed gunman in a matter of minutes. That led people to ask: where now is almighty God? Every tragedy raises the same question. Process theology is honest enough to pronounce that the concept of an all-powerful God is one of the worst mistakes theology has ever made. Some would criticise that while that confronts directly the problem of evil, it creates another problem of how a God lacking omnipotence could create the universe. The answer of process thought is: not by manipulative engineering power, but by another sort of power—the power of persuasive love. This is quite another idea, that the universe is created by persuasion of free creatures and that in the long run is the only power that is creative at all. Omnipotent power could only produce machines.

In contemplating the evolution of the universe Paul Davies (1992) considers the options of no God and the many sorts of God that have been proposed. What comes through 'loud and clear is the fundamental incompatibility of a completely timeless, unchanging, omnipotent God with the notion of creativity in nature, with a universe that can change and evolve and bring forth the genuinely new, a universe in which there is free will' (p. 189). I interpret him as saying that in asking the question, is God necessary? we have to take into account the facts established by science about creativity, indeterminism, degrees of freedom, chance and change. Many concepts of God do not take these facts into account at all. So these concepts of God are incompatible with a modern understanding of the universe in naturalistic terms. Narrow fundamentalism asks of the liberal theist the same rhetorical question of the Grand Inquisitor: why have you come to hinder us?

Paul Davies is not arguing for a proof of the existence of God but that if God there be then such a God would have characteristics consistent with creativity, novelty and freedom of the creation. Indeed he goes further and says, 'I find myself closely in tune with process thought' (p. 192). This is what I want to pursue further in this chapter.

In pursuing the relevance of the concept of God in process thought there is nothing here in the way of proof. What it offers is elucidation through notions which strike more deeply into the root of reality. The way we add to knowledge is by thinking up plausible explanations of hitherto unexplained phenomena and then testing these to see if they work. This is done by further observation and by experimentation (which increases the observable data) where possible.

There is a widespread denial of any kind of cosmic mind. One reason the notion is suspect, as suggested in the lead quotation of this chapter, is by its association with the conception of such a mind in supernaturalistic theism. The argument in this chapter is for a naturalistic concept of cosmic mind consistent with nature as we know it. Here are the propositions. Nothing is supernatural. What is is natural. God is not supernatural. God is natural.

THEISM

There are many theistic doctrines. They can be classified in terms of their answers to five questions asked by Hartshorne and Reese (1953): Is God eternal? Is God temporal? Is God conscious? Does God know the world? Does God include the world? The affirmative answer to these five questions can be symbolised by the following letters:

E Eternal—some aspects of God's reality devoid of change;
T Temporal—some aspects of God's reality capable of change;
C Conscious—self-aware;
K Knowing the World or Universe—omniscient; and
W World-inclusive—having all things as constituents.

If all five components are asserted together (ETCKW) they define the doctrine called panexperientalism promulgated in this chapter. In theistic terms this is the doctrine of panentheism (meaning all in God). God is involved in the world but not identified with the world.

Classical pantheism (e.g., Spinoza) by contrast asserts together only ECKW. God is Eternal Consciousness Knowing and Including the World. God is identified with the World as it now exists. God and World is identical with God. Without T (Temporal) there is no change. The earliest philosophy which functioned as a religion was probably some form of pantheism.

Classical theism (e.g., Augustine, Anselm, Aquinas and much traditional Christianity) asserts together only ECK. God is Eternal Consciousness Knowing but Not Including the World. Such knowledge is deficient because it does not fully and literally contain its objects. The absence of T in ECK is the paradox of a knowledge whose objects change, though the knowledge of these objects does not.

Hartshorne distinguishes a total of eight combinations of these five symbols representing those theistic doctrines that have had some historic importance. For example, in addition to the three major ones above, Plotinus (205–70 CE) recognised God as eternal but beyond consciousness and knowledge, hence represented by E alone. Another example is the limited panexperientalism (ETCK[W]) of William James (1842–1910). Also getting close to panentheism was the temporalistic theism (ETCK) of Socinus' (1539–1604). This is the affirmation of temporality but otherwise makes no change to classical theism. Hence God is subject to change as the world changes. But outside God there is the world. Hence God is less than 'God and the world'. But for the exclusion of the world (W), Socinus would have been a panentheist. Why choose panexperientalism (ETCKW) over any of the other metaphysics? The only answer can be that these other metaphysics have proved inadequate for the spiritual and intellectual needs of humankind, at least in the judgment of those of us who reject a supernaturalistic, mechanistic, interventionist theism such as fundamentalist Christianity.

In theistic panexperientalism (panentheism) God is Eternal, Temporal Consciousness, Knowing and Including the World. What we describe later in this chapter as God's primordial nature is symbolised by E, and God's consequent nature is symbolised by TCKW. God is said to know the world (K) by feeling the feelings of all the subjects composing the world. To know a thing in this sense is to include it. When we say we know a mountain it is entirely outside us. Our knowledge of the mountain is mostly ignorance. There is a sense in which we humans can scarcely be said to have any real knowledge. Real knowledge is to possess. God is said to include the world (W) by being involved in the being of all individual entities. That God knows the world and also includes the world means that God changes as the world changes akin to the way in which we change day by day in our experience, yet nevertheless maintain our identity throughout. To say that God knows a person means that God feels all the feelings, joys and anxieties of that person from moment to moment. None of us has that sort of knowledge.

It may seem to be an omission that the five factors distinguishing the various ideas of God say nothing directly about freedom, persuasion, power, creation, personality and goodness. However, a correct interrelation of the five factors does constitute a definition of divine freedom, power, creation, personality and goodness. This classification of theistic doctrines stresses knowledge and consciousness, not volition and power. Yet it implies a lot about what is a relevant meaning of power. Almighty power is not relevant. Only a conscious being with complete knowledge can use power appropriately and responsibly. As the collect in the introductory rubric for holy communion in the Anglican Prayer Book says, 'unto whom all hearts be open, all desires known, and from whom no secrets are hid'. Only the completely open and responsive one can be trusted with complete responsibility. The power of coercion that humans use to control others is destructive. Paradoxically, love is also power, but of a different sort. There is power in persuasive love. In the long run it is the only power that matters. We have power over the minds of others through the value they may find in our thoughts and feelings. The direct influence of God is analogous, not to the power of a ruler but to the direct power of thought over thought and of feeling over feeling. We have power over others' minds through the value they find in our thoughts and feelings. This is the power of inspiration and suggestion. And so it is with God in process thought. This sort of power could not possibly suppress freedom in the recipients since a minimum of response on their part is supposed. It is not that God makes us be what we are, rather we make ourselves by choosing the good while the source of good perpetually persuades us.

God's power is greater than omnipotence, sheer creation by fiat whose products could only be lifeless machines without individuality. The divine power is fostering the becoming and development of other wills, other powers, other agents endowed with a measure of self-creativity. The ability to foster the becoming and growth of such agents is incomparably greater than sheer fiat. It follows that from the nature of power so analysed, the only alternative to a trivial creation is a tragically dangerous one. For if beings must be self-created, then no providence can prevent them from conflicting with one another, for choices will vary. Freedom of many beings is bound to involve all sorts of risks and in the aggregate the certainty of multitudes of conflicts between incompatible desires. And that is what we see in the world, be it the competition of two youths for the same girl, the demand of one nation against another or the fight between two magpies over the one food morsel. Hence tragedy. In a real sense God is responsible for the tragedy of the world. When Whitehead said 'Life is robbery' and added 'The robber requires justification' (Whitehead 1929a p. 105) he was implying that God had some responsibility for tragedy. As I indicate below, the question is not shall there be tragedy but how does God take tragedy into God's self? A theism that acknowledges tragedy is honest and realistic only if tragedy is not simply external to God but be given a place within the divine life. This is discussed later in this chapter in the context of ultimate meaning.

Panentheism is a brave, imaginative and, for some of us, a compelling concept. By comparison, other views of theism appear truncated, they lack one or other necessary element. Panentheism has a long history in a stream of thought from Ikhnaton in Egypt and Plato in Greece to the present day. At least for me it makes sense of the world I know. There is a meaning to existence. In this view God is not the sculptor or architect working on inanimate material. God is not the potter and we the clay. On the contrary, the material is very much alive and kicking. The cosmic persuasive influence of God can only operate on entities that have their degree of freedom and responsiveness and in responding are transformed. It does not operate with machines. Mechanics operate machines.

THE STORE OF POTENTIALITY IN THE UNIVERSE

This refers to aspects of God's reality devoid of change, represented by the letter E above.

There is the conception amongst materialistic philosophers that reality contains no realm in which possibilities exist as possibilities. This is the nominalist bias that universal values have no independent existence. There is the suggestion in Paul Davies' writings, which is a central proposition in the writings of Whitehead, that from the foundations of the universe its future possibilities were in some form present as potentialities. Another sort of universe might have had different possibilities. But for this universe the possibilities included all that happened and might have happened in cosmic and biological evolution. So at any moment of cosmic and biological evolution, in addition to the past actual world, there are the possibilities of the not yet realised future. These too are real causes. These possibilities are a source of novelty and order. So it is correct to speak of a realm of ordered possibilities. Whitehead conceptualised these possibilities as being in the mind of God. The actualisation of these possibilities was quite limited at any particular time in cosmic history. Only some possibilities are relevant at any particular time. There was no probability at all that human life could have come into existence soon after the big bang. This is the meaning of ordered possibilities. I interpret Paul Davies' phrase, 'we are meant to be here' in this context. Human existence was a possibility from the foundations of the universe. At the appropriate time, 'in the fullness of time', human life did become probable and not just a remote possibility. The idea of the time being ripe or ready is expressed in the Greek word *kairos*. It is not the quantitative time of the clock (*chronos*) but the qualitative time of the occasion, the right time.

In process thought the possibilities or potentialities of the universe are one aspect of the being of God which Whitehead calls the primordial nature of God. Whitehead (1929a) argues that 'the potentiality of the universe must be somewhere' (p. 46) By 'somewhere' Whitehead means 'some actual entity'. He named this entity the primordial nature (mind) of God. It bespeaks a side of the universe which is mental and permanent. It is the idea, 'the same yesterday, and today and for ever' (Hebrews 13:8). This idea is the necessary foundation for understanding what is the ground of novelty in the cosmic history of the universe. The Russian theologian Nicolas Berdyaev said that God created the world through imagination. The imagination referred to is in the primordial mind of God.

The primordial nature of God is conceived as the reservoir of all unrealised potentiality. Yet it is more than a reservoir. The concept includes the notion of the potentialities having within them a lure to the future. The primordial nature of God has a unified aim which is 'the evocation of intensities' (Whitehead 1929a p. 105). What is evoked is the intensity of experience of the individual entities of the universe as they become concretely real in the creation. Apart from this lure to richer experience there could be nothing new in the universe. The primordial nature of God is primordial appetition, else order would be static and remain so. It is a drive in which the permanent passes into and is immanent in the concrete world. The primordial God is 'not *before* all creation, but *with* all creation' (Whitehead 1929a p. 343). God, in God's primordial nature, confronts what is actual in the world with what is possible for it. This is not some kind of determinism, for included in the idea is the degree of freedom of self-constitution of the agents being created.

This concept of God has its parallel in the Platonic idea of a World Soul, *anima mundi*. Plato's world of ideas included all possible values. He regarded the universe as a body animated by the World Soul. The idea of transcendence, that there is something that surpasses empirical reality, is central to the Platonic tradition which was further developed in Christian theology. The relationship of World Soul to God and the world is analogous to that between the human mind and the human body. Whitehead considers that the rest of this aspect of philosophy from Plato onwards are merely footnotes to Plato's genius.

Contemplating the evolution of novelty in the cosmos is one avenue that leads to the question, is God necessary? The response of process thought is that the existence of real novelty and freedom leads to asking what is behind the phenomena and then discovering the relevance of a concept of God that includes the potentialities of existence. A desperate need of our time is for a faith that can direct a person's commitment to the creative source of all good of all creatures as it works in the temporal world.

THE MEANING OF IT ALL

There is a second avenue in this argument that comes more directly from human experience in contemplating our own lives. Philosopher Bryan Magee (1997 p. 240) in the midst of his busy life considered himself to have had a mid-life crisis. It came in the form of deep disquiet about the meaning of life. Did his life and that of anyone else have meaning? Was there anything about life that was enduring despite the inevitability of death? Confronted with the possible meaninglessness of everything he felt not just horror but an existential terror of nothingness.

> Quite apart from any consideration of self: politics, business and the professions were in themselves nothing, and the daily life and work of the world just a lot of meaningless vanity. People busied themselves in offices and factories, or hurried to and fro between these and their homes; markets and concourses teemed with crowds, traffic crammed the streets, buses and trains ran, airplanes flew, telephones rang; everywhere there was bustle and noise, strain and striving, people jostling and worrying and getting ill, pursuing leisure, pleasure and possessions as frantically as they worked. And to what end ultimately? None at all. In fact, whether they realised it or not, they were just doing these things repetitively for their own sakes, and would go on doing so until they and everything else disappeared in total darkness ... even on their own terms the politics and business of the world were absurdly evanescent. (pp. 266–7)

Magee seemed to have reached a depth of despair which comes when all that seems to give hope to human existence is seen to be an illusion. He is not the first person to have such experiences. The book of Ecclesiastes is the story of a great king of Israel who had tasted just about everything that life had to offer. Wealth?—No-one could exceed him in luxurious lifestyle. Wisdom?—His was world renowned. Fame?—He was a king, the most famous man of his time.

Systematically he sampled all of life's powers and pleasures, yet all left him bitterly disappointed. All proved meaningless. What is the point of life? You work hard, someone else gets the credit. You struggle to be good, and evil people take advantage of you. You seek pleasure and it turns sour on you. And everyone, rich or poor, good or evil, meets the same end. We all die. There is only one word to describe this life: meaningless! 'Meaningless! Meaningless!' Ooheleth said. 'Everything is meaningless' (Ecclesiastes 12:8).

Magee's immediate response to his particular crisis of meaning was to change his lifestyle so that he concentrated on those experiences that meant most to him such as music and intimate human relationships. It meant changing his job and spending much more time philosophising about his life and that of the world. This gave him a modicum of relief. But he never found any answer to the apparent meaninglessness of life for him.

Life is meaningless if all we see are isolated experiences like separated islands in an ocean. Nothing connects them in a meaningful whole. This is life at high tide where meaning evaporates into separate islands and life is reduced to trivialisation. At the flood of high tide much disappears and things are studied in isolation; we separate science and religion and the human from the non-human part of the world. What appear to be islands in an ocean at the flood of high tide are at low tide shown to be one. All are connected one with each other by the sea floor. To ignore this connection is to confuse what islands really are with what at first sight they appear to be.

There can be no response to the question of the meaning of life if we leave our own life out. Schopenhauer described materialism as the philosophy of the subject who forgets to take account of himself. To take account of oneself is to ask: what value am I if in the end I account for nothing? Alternatively: how could I possibly account for something in the long history of the universe that eventually fizzes out? The question of the meaning of human life leads directly in process thought to what Whitehead called the consequent nature of God. This is a philosophy of what endures or what is permanent in a seemingly non-permanent universe. Material permanence is not a *sine qua non* for value.

A CONSEQUENCE OF EXISTING

God is not only the persuader of existence in God's primordial nature. God is also a consequence of the whole history of the cosmos. God is the end and the beginning. God acts in the world by persuasion through God's primordial nature and responds to the world with compassion in God's consequent nature (TCKW). The final real facts which constitute that history are not to be thought of as substances but as occasions of experience from the experience of being a proton to that of being a person. Our own human experience suggests that view. The real facts of our lives are the experiences that make each one of us a person. In God's consequent nature God experiences all the experiences, all the joys and all the sorrows of all creation of all time. God's memory of the richness of experience of the universe grows as the universe evolves. God must have been different after the big bang and even more so after the evolution of humankind. Thus our experience from moment to moment 'enriches the divine life'. This is the ultimate meaning of existence. God feels with unique adequacy the feelings of all subjects composing the world and retains these feelings forever. God is not like us separated from a past which we have largely forgotten. Nothing of value is forgotten or lost in the divine nature.

Contrasted with this view of God's feelings for the world is the classical theism of Aristotle who said that God is mover of all things, unmoved by any. At the opposite extreme is the polytheistic view in Greek mythology whose gods are capable of all sorts of emotions; they are jealous, easily offended and sexually desirous. The concept of the consequent nature of God is a mediating view. God feels all the feelings of all subjects but without inferior emotions, except as vicariously participated.

Whereas it is true to say that in God's primordial nature God creates the world, it is also true to say that in God's consequent nature the world creates God. This is the doctrine of objective immortality. Our immediate actions eventually perish but yet they live for evermore in the divine memory. This idea that our existence from moment to moment enriches the divine life is part of a stream of thought which stretches at least as far back as Plato and parts of the Judeo-Christian Scriptures, through Schelling, Fechner, C. S. Peirce, Berdyaev, William James, Buber, Radhakrishnan, Iqbal, Tillich and Whitehead (Hartshorne & Reese 1953). It became lost in much of the tradition of classical theism.

Some interpreters find suggestions of Whitehead's concept of the consequent nature of God in Plato's concept of the World Soul. I have already indicated that for Plato the world was animated by the World Soul which worked as a persuasive not a coercive influence. But the World Soul is also created by the creation. In this sense Plato's God anticipates not only Whitehead's primordial nature of God but also the consequent nature of God (Hartshorne 1984 p. 53).

Everything we do makes a difference to God. This is true of the lesser creatures also. God will never be the same again because we have lived and because they also have lived. So what we do, what we affirm, what we choose, how we deal with meaninglessness make a permanent difference to God. We fade but God does not. A friend whose daughter recently tragically died in the flower of her youth told me that he was greatly supported in his grief by this understanding.

At the end of the Russian Orthodox service for the dead, the choir and mourners join together in singing the *Viechnaya Pamyat*. The words mean eternal memory. The memory in question is God's. David Bromell, the minister of the Durham Street Methodist church in Christchurch, New Zealand, talked to the children at a service about this aspect of God being like a balloon (Bromell 1997). The children blew up their balloons. We add something to God out of our own breath and life and God becomes bigger, brighter and greater. All that we value in our lives, he said, is valued by God, and adds value to God. Present at that service was a little boy Andrew who was very sick with leukaemia. Two weeks later Andrew died. At his funeral Andrew's parents took the balloon in a box to the graveside. They cut the ribbon and watched the balloon soar into the heavens. Those gathered at the graveside sang the following hymn composed by Professor Colin Gibson of the University of Otago:

> Nothing is lost on the breath of God,
> nothing is lost forever;
> God's breath is love, and that love will remain,
> holding the world forever.
> No feather too light, no hair too fine,
> no flower too brief in its glory;
> no drop in the ocean, no dust in the air,
> but is counted and told in God's story.
>
> Nothing is lost on the breath of God,
> nothing is lost forever;
> God sees with love, and that love will remain,
> holding the world forever.
> No journey too far, no distance too great,
> no valley of darkness too blinding;
> no creature too humble, no child too small
> for God to be seeking and finding.
>
> Nothing is lost on the breath of God,
> nothing is lost forever;
> God's heart is love, and that love will remain,
> holding the world forever.
> No impulse of love, no office of care,
> no moment of life in its fullness;
> no beginning too late, no ending too soon,
> but is gathered and known in God's goodness.

A PERSONAL REFLECTION ON THE CONVERGENCE OF BIOLOGY AND FAITH

The meaning of life has, for me, both a religious and a scientific foundation. First came a religious awareness which led me to simplified answers to the meaning of life. It provided for me a harmony in simplicity. Later on science showed me that the world was more complicated. That led me to distrust the simplicity that had yet been so important for me. Could I find a harmony in the new diversity that confronted me? A major problem was that the science I was becoming familiar with as I became a practising scientist presented me with a mechanistic universe. And that provided no clues to my most fundamental experiences. It had nothing to say about my feelings, which were for me the most important part of my life. I knew the truth 'I feel therefore I am'. How did feelings come into a mechanical universe? This question is now a central one for the inventors of artificial intelligence. Can the creators of robots that have artificial intelligence create a robot that has feelings? In the language of their discourse, what is missing is qualia, which is the experiential quality of sensations. This is what robots lack. They do not know what it is like to taste, to experience the redness of an apple or the intimate feelings of love of another person.

The gap I was discovering between what science described and what I experience started me on a new journey of discovery. It began with my reading Whitehead's (1925) *Science and the Modern World*. I felt this was written for me, especially chapter 5, 'The Romantic Reaction'. The first paragraph of this chapter contained this statement: 'the contemporary scheme of science exhibited man as helpless to co-operate with the irresistible mechanism of nature'. Whitehead said we were in the grip of two attitudes that are inconsistent. A scientific realism based on mechanism is conjoined with an unwavering belief that humankind and the higher animals are self-determining organisms. Science seemed to say their lives are set on deterministic pathways. Commonsense said they had a degree of self-determination. Furthermore, if there is a God of the mechanistic universe that God can only be a mechanic. Hume had already said that in response to Paley's arguments for God as the designer of nature. The only way of mitigating mechanism, said Whitehead, is to discover that the universe is not a mechanism.

In chapter 5 of *Science and the Modern World* Whitehead argued that much light was shed on the distracting inconsistency in modern thought by English poets, particularly Milton, Wordsworth and Tennyson. Wordsworth felt that something had been left out and what had been left out was everything that was most important. It was the problem of mechanism that appalled these poets:

'The stars,' she whispers,' blindly run.'

This line from Tennyson's *In Memoriam* states starkly the whole philosophic problem implicit in the poem. Each molecule blindly runs. The human body is a collection of molecules. The human body blindly runs. There is no escape from the mechanistic conclusion. Mental states are irrelevant in human actions. Wordsworth's characteristic thought is summed up in the line:

We murder to dissect.

The important facts of nature elude the scientific method because its model of nature is an abstraction from reality. Wordsworth scorns the man whom he accuses of peeping and botanising on his mother's grave.

On reading Whitehead, who so clearly set before me the dilemma of feelings in a mechanistic universe, my mind flashed back to a lecture I had heard as an undergraduate in the University of Melbourne. It was given to the student's Science Society by W. E. Agar, the professor of zoology. The subject was the philosophy of biology. I hardly understood a word of the lecture but enough must have sunk in for me to recall much later on that Professor Agar was interested in a Whiteheadian interpretation of biology. So I wrote from where I then was in the University of Adelaide, asking Agar what should I now read. He replied that I should read Charles Hartshorne's recently published *The Philosophy and Psychology of Sensation*. He added that he had just completed a book on a Whiteheadian interpretation of biology which he modestly entitled *A Contribution to the Theory of the Living Organism*. Its first sentence read: 'The main thesis of this book is that all living organisms are subjects'. That is what I needed to know. How was a biology, which looked on organisms as objects, to be reconciled with the idea of organisms as feelings subjects? Agar had come to accept mentality, self-determination, feelings and sentience as real and not just epiphenomena. Moreover, he identified three areas of biology that seemed resistant to a completely mechanistic analysis: developmental biology, animal behaviour and evolution. To this day, at least for some of us, these three areas of biology still defy a completely mechanistic analysis. This is not to say that the mechanistic analysis has not been profitable. It has. It has led in our time to all we know about molecular biology. But it leaves out the subjective aspect of life.

Professor Agar was a brilliant cell biologist and also a student of animal behaviour. He was educated in King's College, Cambridge, and at the age of thirty-eight was elected a fellow of the Royal Society. His book initiated my exploration of biology in the light of Whitehead's system of thought. Much later I was to find similar fellow feeling with the geneticist and development biologist Professor C. H. Waddington. He told me on one occasion while we browsed in a bookshop in Rome that as an undergraduate in Cambridge he had read all the works of Whitehead. This had, he said, greatly influenced both the problems he chose to work on and the manner in which he tried to solve them. His work is a fine demonstration of how a scientist's metaphysical convictions influenced his science. Mechanists usually deny that their mechanistic conviction influences their science. It does. But to admit it would be to admit that science is not completely objective.

As for myself, as a graduate student, besides reading as much of Whitehead and Hartshorne as I could, I also read the dialogues of Plato as being highly relevant to an understanding of an organic as opposed to a mechanistic concept of nature. It was fortunate for me that my biological interests in ecology took me to the University of Chicago in the 1940s. It was not only a world centre of ecology but also, unknown to me at the time, the world centre of Whiteheadian thought. Besides having Charles Hartshorne in the philosophy department (which also included the logical positivist Rudolf Carnap) there was in the divinity school a veritable galaxy of Whiteheadian theologians. They included, Henry Nelson Wieman, Bernard Meland, Bernard Loomer and Daniel Day Williams. To add yet more to these riches, the most distinguished professor in the department of zoology (who was actually called 'distinguished professor') where I was doing research was Sewall Wright. He was one of four founding fathers of the neo-Darwinian synthesis of evolution, the others being Ronald Fisher, J. B. S. Haldane and Theodosius Dobzhansky. Just as important was the fact that Sewall Wright was convinced of a panexperientalist view of the world. He was a close friend of Charles Hartshorne but seemed to have worked out his philosophy independently. I recall that he found the idea of God's feeling the world immediately in all its experiences problematical because of the vast distances involved. I suspect that is probably less of a problem in the physics of today. In 1953 he gave the presidential address to the American Society of Naturalists, which published a leading journal for evolutionary and ecological studies, *The American Naturalist*. Sewall Wright's address was titled 'Gene and Organism' and was published in that journal. It was a closely argued case for the gene as an organism and therefore a subject and not a mere object. Wright took into account what were the beginnings of molecular biology, which some of Wright's colleagues even then called by that name. That was appropriate because of the complex relationships of atoms and molecules that go into making a living organism.

Having discovered Chicago's biology and theology in those heady days I asked Hartshorne who else I should know. He replied immediately, 'my most brilliant student, John Cobb'. I should add that Hartshorne had many brilliant students such as Martin Gardner, Richard Rorty, Schubert Ogden and Huston Smith, some of whose work developed in different avenues from that of Hartshorne. John Cobb was, and still is, director of the Center for Process Studies in Claremont, California. My friendship with him and with David Griffin, also a director of the Center, led us to work together on process thought and biology. This led to a consultation at Villa Serbelloni (of the Rockefeller Foundation) in Bellagio, Italy, in 1974 and the book *Mind in Nature* (Cobb & Griffin 1977). Later Cobb and I wrote *The Liberation of Life: From the Cell to the Community* (Birch & Cobb 1981). David Griffin's excursions into biology include his important book *Unsnarling the World-Knot: Consciousness, Freedom and the Mind–Body Problem* (Griffin 1998) which confronts the subjective head on.

My researches in the ecological aspects of evolution brought me to work in the laboratory of the geneticist and evolutionist Theodosius Dobzhansky at Columbia University in New York. We later worked together for a year in Brazil and after that for a year in Sydney. Dobzhansky was a strict Darwinian and famous a such, particularly for his book *Genetics and the Origin of Species*. His most brilliant student was Richard Lewontin. The three of us had many discussions on Whitehead. All the time lurking in the background of Dobzhansky's thought was his upbringing in Russia in the Russian Orthodox Church. How to link the two? That was a problem for him when we first met. He was not enthusiastic about the synthesis of science and religion I was discovering through the thought of Whitehead. He charged me with believing that atoms had brains! He was more interested in the synthesis of Teilhard de Chardin, who was both palaeontologist and priest. Dobzhansky was drawn to Teilhard's Omega notion to which all things were supposed to move. But he rejected 'the within of things', which was the one aspect of Teilhard that I liked.

I persuaded Dobzhansky to come to some lectures of Paul Tillich in New York that I was attending. He became attracted to Tillich's concept of 'ultimate concern'. This phrase was essentially

Tillich's synonym for God. Most of our concerns are secondary. But there are some concerns that are of ultimate importance because they fulfil human life. In the biblical story of Martha and Mary the concerns of Martha were secondary. Mary's were of ultimate concern. Dobzhansky asked how could human concern for the ultimate that fulfilled human life have evolved? He was in fact facing up to the reality of the subjective about which Darwinian evolution had little, if anything, to say.

Dobzhansky's pursuit of this question resulted in his book *The Biology of Ultimate Concern*. Dobzhansky (1967) argued that the subjective, such as mentality, emerged at a some stage in the evolution of mammals. Go back much further and it doesn't exist. I argued for the opposite: that the subjective did not emerge out of nothing at some stage of evolution but that the subjective was present in some form all the way down to protons, quarks and whatever you have at that low level of organisation. We remained to differ on this subject, as is evident in Dobzhansky's (1956) book *The Biological Basis of Human Freedom*. In Dobzhansky's scheme, freedom and self-determination are late arrivals in evolution. I argued that in some elementary form they must have been present in the ultimate physical building blocks of the universe. In our philosophical pursuits neither Dobzhansky nor I got much support from the leading evolutionists of the day such as Ernst Mayr and G. G. Simpson who were close friends of Dobzhansky and strictly mechanistic in their evolutionary biology.

The big divide between biologists who philosophise about their subject is that between those who see living organisms primarily as machines (objects) and those who see them as subjects as well as objects. Dobzhansky and I agreed that living organisms were subjects as well as objects but Dobzhansky, like most biologists I know, could not accept the idea of a subjective in the non- biological world. And his concept of God was more interventionist than mine. I have thought it important in this book to indicate a diversity of views while at the same time giving reasons why I accept a panexperiental-ist and panentheistic view as coming closest to the reality I know. For me it is a revelation. It is my yes to life. I hope it might be that for others as well. The former secretary-general of the United Nations, Dag Hammarskjold (1964 p. 169) put it this way:

> I don't know Who—or what—put the question, I don't know when it was put. I don't even remembering answering. But at some moment I did answer Yes to Someone—or Something—and from that hour I was certain that existence is meaningful and that, therefore, my life, in self-surrender had a goal.

REFERENCES

Ammons, A. R. (1999) Birds of a Feather *New Scientist* 2170: 30–3.

Andrewartha, H. G. & L. C. Birch (1954) *The Distribution and Abundance of Animals* Chicago: University of Chicago Press.

Andrewartha, H. G. & L. C. Birch (1984) *The Ecological Web* Chicago: University of Chicago Press.

Australian Academy of Science (1999) *On Human Cloning: A Position Statement* Canberra: AAS.

Barlow, Kenneth (1988) *Recognising Health* London: The Garrison Society.

Baruss, I. E. & R. J. Moore (1998) Beliefs About Consciousness and Reality of Participants at 'Tucson II' *Journal of Consciousness Studies* 5: 483–96.

Birch, Charles (1993a) *Regaining Compassion: For Humanity and Nature* Sydney: UNSW Press.

Birch, Charles (1993b) *Confronting the Future: Australia and the World: The Next Hundred Years* Ringwood, Victoria: Penguin.

Birch, Charles (1995) *Feelings* Sydney: UNSW Press.

Birch, Charles, & Paul Abrecht (eds) (1975) *Genetics and the Quality of Life* Sydney: Pergamon Press.

Birch, Charles, & John B. Cobb (1981) *The Liberation of Life: From the Cell to the Community* Cambridge: Cambridge University Press. Reprinted (1990) Denton, TX: Environmental Ethics Books.

Birch, Charles, & Lukas Vischer (1997) *Living With the Animals: The Community of God's Creatures* Geneva: World Council of Churches.

Birch, L. C. & P. R. Ehrlich (1967) The Balance of Nature and Population Control *American Naturalist* 101: 73–98.

Boden, Margaret (1996) *The Philosophy of Artificial Life* Oxford: Oxford University Press.

Bohr, Niels (1958) *Physical Science and the Problem of Life* New York: Wiley.

Bonner, John Tyler (1983) Chemical Signals of Social Amoebae *Scientific American* 248: 106–12.

Bromell David J. (1997) Processing Towards Death *Creative Transformation* 7(2): 6–9.

Brooks, Harvey (1978) The Problem of Research Priorities *Daedalus: Journal of the American Academy of Arts and Sciences* 107(2): 171–90.

Brown, Lester (1991) *State of the World 1991: A Worldwatch Institute Report on Progress Towards a Sustainable Society* New York: W. W. Norton.

Brown, Lester (1998) *State of the World 1998: A Worldwatch Institute Report on Progress Towards a Sustainable Society* New York: W. W. Norton.

Brown, Lester (1999) *State of the World 1999: A Worldwatch Institute Report on Progress Towards a Sustainable Society* New York: W. W. Norton.

Bruyns, Noel (17 February 1999) Develop Your Souls, Nelson Mandela Tells South Africans *Bulletin* Geneva: Ecumenical News International.

Capra, Fritjof (1996) *The Web of Life* London: HarperCollins.

Cobb, John B. (1982) *Beyond Dialogue: Toward a Mutual Transformation of Christianity and Buddhism* Philadelphia: Fortress Press.

Cobb, John B. & David Ray Griffin (eds) (1977) *Mind in Nature: Essays on the Interface of Science and Philosophy* Washington, DC: University Press of America.

Cornwell, John (ed.) (1998) *Consciousness and Human Identity* Oxford: Oxford University Press.

Coveney, Peter & Roger Highfield (1995) *Frontiers of Complexity: The Search for Order in a Chaotic World* London: Faber & Faber.

Covey, Stephen R. (1989) *The 7 Habits of Highly Effective People* New York: Business Library.

Curtis, Lionel (1938) *Civitas Dei: The Commonwealth of God* London: Macmillan.

Daly, Herman E. & J. B. Cobb (1989) *For the Common Good: Rediscovering the Economy Toward Community, the Environment and a Sustainable Future* Boston: Beacon Press.

Darwin, Charles (1859) *On the Origin of Species: By Means of Natural Selection*. Reprint (1901) New York: Ward, Lock & Co.

Davies, Paul (1989) *The Cosmic Blueprint* London: Unwin Paperbacks.

Davies, Paul (1992) *The Mind of God: Science and the Search for Ultimate Meaning* London: Simon & Schuster.

Davies, Paul (1998) *The Fifth Miracle: The Search for the Origin of Life* Ringwood, Victoria: Penguin Books .

Davies, Paul & John Gribbin (1991) *The Matter Myth: Towards Twenty-First-Century Science* London: Viking.

Dawkins, Richard (1998) *Unweaving the Rainbow* London: Allen Lane, Penguin Press.

Diamond, Jarred (1993) New Guineans and Their Natural World. In Stephen Kellert and E. O. Wilson (eds),*The Biophilia Hypothesis* Washington, DC: Island Press.

Diamond, Jared (1998) *Guns, Germs and Steel: A Short History of Everybody for the Last 13,000 Years* London: Vintage.

Dobzhansky, Th. (1956) *The Biological Basis of Human Freedom* New York: Columbia University Press.

Dobzhansky, Th. (1967) *The Biology of Ultimate Concern* New York: New American Library.

Dover, Gabriel A. (1996) On the Edge *Nature* 365: 704–6.

Eckersley, Richard (1998a) Perspectives and Progress. In Richard Eckersley (ed.), *Measuring Progress* (pp. 3–34) Canberra: CSIRO.

Eckersley, Richard (1998b) Redefining Progress: Shaping the Future of Human Needs *Family Matters* 51: 6–12

Eckersley, Richard (1999) Richard Eckersley Replies *Family Matters* 52: 44–6.

Eddington, A. S. (1928) *The Nature of the Physical World* Cambridge: Cambridge University Press.

Ehrlich, Paul R. (1997) *A World of Wounds: Ecologists and the Human Dilemma* Olderdorf/Luhe, Germany: Ecology Institute Press.

Ehrlich, Paul & Anne Ehrlich (1981) *Extinction: The Causes and Consequences of Disappearance of Species* New York: Random House.

Epstein, Helen (16 July 1998) Life and Death on the Social Ladder *New York Review of Books* (pp. 26–30).

Feynman, Richard P. (1998) *The Meaning of it All* New York: Allen Lane, Penguin Press.

Frankl, V. E. (1969) Reductionism and Nihilism. In Arthur Koestler & S. R. Smythies (eds), *Beyond Reductionism: New Perspectives on the Life Sciences* (pp. 396–427) London: Hutchinson.

Franks. Nigel R. (1989) Army Ants: A Collective Intelligence *Scientific American* (pp. 139–45).

Gardner, Martin (1996) *The Night is Large: Collected Essays, 1938–1995* London: Penguin Books.

Garton Ash, Timothy (1997) *File: A Personal History* London: HarperCollins.

Gilbert, Martin (1997) *Holocaust Journey: Travelling in Search of the Past* London: Phoenix.

Goodenough, Ursula (1998) *The Sacred Depths of Nature* New York: Oxford University Press.

Goodfield, June (1972) The Problem of Reduction in Biology *Nature* 240: 446–8.

Goodwin, Brian (1994) *How the Leopard Changed its Spots* London: Phoenix Giant Paperback.

Goodwin, Brian (1998) All for One *New Scientist* 2138: 32–5.

Gordon, Deborah M. (1996) The Organization of Work in Social Insect Colonies *Nature* 380: 121–4.

Gould, Stephen Jay (1977) *Ever Since Darwin* New York: W. W. Norton.

Gould, Stephen Jay (1981) *The Mismeasure of Man* New York: W. W. Norton.

Gould, Stephen Jay (1987) *An Urchin in the Storm* New York: W. W. Norton

Gould, Stephen Jay (1996) *Life's Grandeur* London: Jonathan Cape.

Griffin, David Ray (1998) *Unsnarling the World-Knot: Consciousness, Freedom and the Mind–Body Problem* Los Angeles and Berkeley: University of California Press.

Hagan, P. & M. Cohen (1981) Diffused-Induced Metamorphosis in Dictyostelium *Journal of Theoretical Biology* 37: 881–909.

Hamilton, Clive & Hugh Saddler (1997) *The Genuine Progress Indicator for Australia* Canberra: Australian Institute Discussion Paper no 14.

Hamilton, Edith (1952) *The Greek Way to Western Civilisation* New York: Mentor Books.

Hammarskjold, Dag (1964) *Markings* London: Faber & Faber.
Hartshorne, Charles (1984) *Omnipotence and Other Theological Mistakes* Albany, NY: State University of New York Press.
Hartshorne, Charles (1987) *Wisdom and Moderation: A Philosophy of the Middle Way* Albany, NY: State University of New York Press.
Hartshorne, Charles (1997) *The Zero Fallacy and Other Essays in Neoclassical Philosophy* La Salle, IL: Open Court.
Hartshorne, Charles & William L. Reese (1953) *Philosophers Speak of God* Chicago: University of Chicago Press.
Havel, Vaclev (1998) The State of the Republic. *New York Review of Books* 45 (4):42–6.
Holmes, Bob (1998) Life is ... *New Scientist* 2138 (pp. 38–42).
Hutchins, Robert M. (1968) *The Learning Society* Harmondsworth, Middlesex: Penguin.
Jones, Steve (1997a) Why is Sex Fun: The Evolution of Human Sexuality *New York Review of Books* 54(12): 39–41.
Jones, Steve (1997b) *In the Blood: God, Genes and Destiny* London: Flamingo, HarperCollins.
Josselson Ruthellen (1996) *The Space Between Us: Exploring the Dimensions of Human Relationships* Thousand Oaks, CA: Sage Publications.
Kauffman, Stuart A. (1993) *The Origins of Order: Self-Organization and Selection in Evolution* Oxford: Oxford University Press.
Kauffman, Stuart A. (1995) *At Home in the Universe: The Search for Laws of Complexity* London: Viking.
Kitcher, Philip (1997) *The Lives to Come: The Genetic Revolution and Human Possibilities* Harmondsworth, Middlesex: Penguin.
Kornfield, Jack (1988) *A Part With Heart* London: Rider.
Kurzwell, Ray (1998) *The Age of Spiritual Machines: When Computers Exceed Human Intelligence* New York: Viking.
Langmore, John (September 1995) Preserving Biological Diversity *The Australia Institute* 5 (pp. 3–4).
Lawrence, Michael (10 September 1997) How Liveware Can Limit the Future *The Australian*.
Levine, Joseph & David T. Suzuki (1998) *The Secret of Life: Redesigning the Living World* New York: W. H. Freeman.
Levins, Richard & Richard Lewontin (1985) *The Dialectical Biologist* Cambridge, MA: Harvard University Press.
Lewontin, R. C. (1991) *Biology as Ideology: The Doctrine of DNA* New York: Harper Perennial.
Lewontin, Richard (1996) The Last of the Nasties *New York Review of Books* 43(4): 20–6.
Lewontin, R. C. (1998a) Survival of the Nicest *New York Review of Books* 45(16): 59–62.
Lewontin, R. C. (1998b) The Confusion Over Cloning. In Gregory A. Pence (ed.), *Flesh of My Flesh: The Ethics of Human Cloning* (pp. 129–39) Lanham, MD: Rowman & Littlefield.
Lewontin, R. C., Stephen Rose & Leon J. Kamin (1984) *Not in Our Genes: Biology, Ideology and Human Nature* New York: Pantheon.
Litvin, Daniel (21 March 1998) Dirt Poor *The Economist*.

Livingstone, R. W. (1915) *Greek Genius and its Meaning to Us* Oxford: Oxford University Press.

Livingstone, R. W. (1935) *Greek Ideals and Modern Life* Oxford: Oxford University Press.

Livingstone, R. W. (1944) *Plato and Modern Education*. The Bede Lecture. Cambridge: Cambridge University Press.

Magee, Bryan (1997) *Confessions of a Philosopher* London: Weidenfeld & Nicholson.

Maslow, Abraham (1971) *The Farther Reaches of Human Nature* New York: Viking.

Maynard Smith, John (2 March 1995) Life on the Edge of Chaos *New York Review of Books* (pp. 28–30).

Maynard Smith, John (1998) *Shaping Life: Genes, Embryos and Evolution* London: Weidenfeld & Nicholson.

McDaniel, Jay B. (1986) Christian Spirituality as Openness to Fellow Creatures *Environmental Ethics* 8(1): 33–46.

McDaniel, Jay B. (1989) *Of God and Pelicans: A Theory of Reverence for Life* Louisville, KY: Westminster/Knox.

McGinn, Colin (3 January 1999) Hello, Hal *New York Times Book Review* (pp. 11–2).

Michnik, Adam (14 January 1999) A Death in St Petersburg *New York Review of Books* (pp. 4–6).

Midgley, Mary (1992) *Science as Salvation: A Modern Myth and its Meaning* London: Routledge.

Midgley, Mary (1996) One World but a Big One *Journal of Consciousness Studies* 3: 500–14.

Monk, Ray (1997) *Bertrand Russell: The Spirit of Solitude* London: Vintage.

Murphy, Michael P. & A. S. O'Neill (eds) (1995) *What is Life? The Next Fifty Years: Speculations on the Future of Biology* Cambridge: Cambridge University Press.

Myers, David G. & Ed Diener (1996) The Pursuit of Happiness *Scientific American* 7(1): 40–3.

Nabham, Gary P. (1997) Cultural Parallels in Viewing North American Habitats. In Michael E. Soule and Gary Leach (eds), *Reinventing Nature: Responses to Postmodern Deconstruction* (pp. 87–101) Washington, DC: Island Press.

Nagel, Thomas (1974) What is it Like to be a Bat? *Philosophical Review* 83: 435–50. Reprinted in Thomas Nagel (1979) *Mortal Questions* Cambridge: Cambridge University Press.

Nagel, Thomas (1986) *The View from Nowhere* New York: Oxford University Press.

Needham, Joseph (1943) *Time the Refreshing River* London: Allen & Unwin.

Niebuhr, Reinhold (1966) World Community and World Government. In Wayne H. Cowan (ed.), *Witness to a Generation* (pp. 29–31) New York: Bobbs-Merrill.

Niebuhr, Reinhold (1969) The King's Chapel and the King's Court. Reprinted in Leon Howell & Vivien Lindermayer (eds) (1991) *Ethics in the Present Tense* (pp. 208–10) New York: Friendship Press.

Pagels, Elaine (1988) *Adam, Eve and the Serpent* New York: Random House.

Paglia Camille (5 May 1991) Ninnies, Pedants, Tyrants and Other Academics *New York Review of Books* (pp. 28–33).

Passmore, John (1970) *The Perfectibility of Man* London: Duckworth.

Pearse, I. H. (1979) *The Quality of Life: The Peckham Approach to Human Ethology* Edinburgh: Scottish Academic Press.

Pence, G. E. (ed.) (1998) *Flesh of my Flesh* London: Rowan and Littlefield.

Picket, S. T. A. & P. S. White (1985) *The Ecology of Natural Disturbance and Patch Dynamics* Orlando, FL: Academic Press.

Powell, S. (22 October 1997) Stress: The Distressing News *The Australian*.

Prigogine, Ilya & Isabelle N. Stengers (1984) *Order out of Chaos: Man's New Dialogue with Nature* New York: Bantam.

Rathbone, Christina (1997) *On the Outside Looking In: A Year in an Inner-City High School* New York: Atlantic Monthly Press.

Resnick, Mitchell (1995) Learning About Life. In Christopher Langton (ed.), *Artificial Life: An Overview* (pp. 229–441) Cambridge, MA: MIT Press.

Ridley Matt (1998) *The Origins of Virtue: Human Instincts and the Evolution of Cooperation* London: Penguin.

Rifkin, Jeremy (1998) *A Biotech Century: Harnessing the Gene and Remaking the World* New York: Tarcher/Putnam.

Rose, Steven (April 1998) The Genetics of Blame *New Internationalist* 300 (pp. 20–1).

Schrodinger, E. D. (1944) *What is Life? The Physical Aspects of the Living Cell* Cambridge: Cambridge University Press.

Searle, John R. (1997) Consciousness and the Philosophers *New York Review of Books* 44(4): 43–50.

Semler, Ricardo (1994) *Maverick! The Success Story Behind the World's Most Unusual Workplace* London: Arrow books.

Sennett, Richard (1998) *The Corrosion of Character: The Personal Consequences of Work in the New Capitalism* New York: W. W. Norton.

Shermer, M. (2 January 1999) Give us Our Wings *Sydney Morning Herald*.

Singer, Peter (1993) *How Are We to Live? Ethics in an Age of Self-Interest* Melbourne: Text.

Singer, Peter (17 June 1998) New Ideas for the Evolutionary Left *The Australian*.

Sokal, Alan & Jean Bricmont (1998) *Intellectual Impostures: Postmodern Philosophers' Abuse of Science* London: Profile.

Soule, Michael E. (1995) The Social Siege of Nature. In Michael E. Soule & Gary Leach (eds), *Reinventing Nature: Responses to Postmodern Deconstruction* (pp. 137–70) Washington, DC: Island Press.

Stapp, H. P. (1993) *Mind, Matter and Quantum Mechanics* Berlin: Springer-Verlag.

Stewart, Ian (1998) *Life's Other Secret: The New Mathematics of the Living World* London: Allen Lane.

Storr, Anthony (1997) *Feet of Clay: A Study of Gurus* London: HarperCollins.

Szent-Gyorgy, Albert (1972) *The Living State: With Observations on Cancer* New York: Academic Press.

Tillich, Paul (1956) *The Religious Situation* New York: Meridian.

Waddington, C. H. (1969) The Practical Consequences of Metaphysical Beliefs on a Biologist's Work: An Autobiographical Note. In C. H. Waddington (ed.),*Towards a Theoretical Biology. 2. Sketches* (pp. 72–81) Edinburgh: Edinburgh University Press.

Weinburg, Steven (1977) *The First Three Minutes* London: Andre Deutsch.

Whitehead, A. N. (1925) *Science and the Modern World* Cambridge: Cambridge University Press. Reprinted (1967) New York: Free Press.

Whitehead, A. N. (1929a) *Process and Reality* London: Macmillan. Corrected edition David Ray Griffin & Donald W. Shelbourne (eds) (1978) New York: Free Press.

Whitehead, A. N. (1929b) *The Function of Reason* Boston: Beacon.

Whitehead, A. N. (1938) *Modes of Thought* New York: Free Press.

Williamson, G. Scott & I. H. Pearse (1931) *The Case for Action* London: Faber & Faber.

Wilson, E. O. (1978) *On Human Nature* Cambridge, MA: Harvard University Press.

Wilson, E. O. (1994) *Naturalist* London: Penguin Books.

Wilson, E. O.(1998) *Consilience: The Unity of Knowledge* New York: Knopf.

Wolpert, Lewis (1999) *Malignant Sadness* London: Faber & Faber.

Wolpert, Lewis & Alison Richards (1997) *Passionate Minds: The Inner World of Scientists* Oxford: Oxford University Press.

Wood, W. B. (1987) Virus Assembly and its Genetic Control. In F. E. Yates (ed.), *Self-Organizing Systems: The Emergence of Order* New York: Plenum.

World Council of Churches (1982) *Manipulating Life: Ethical Issues in Genetic Engineering* Geneva: WCC.

World Wide Fund for Nature (1998) *Living Planet Report 1998* Geneva: WWFN.

Worster, Donald (1997) Nature and the Disorder of History. In Michael A. Soule and Gary Leach (eds), *Reinventing Nature: Responses to Postmodern Deconstruction* (pp. 65–85) Washington, DC: Island Press.

INDEX